On Gravel Roads

M Jeannie Irwin
Henderson

On Gravel Roads

Dedicated to Jean and Allan Irwin who gave us a childhood worth remembering.

Special thanks to my brothers Robin, Ross, Lanny and John Bruce for sharing their stories and their childhood with me. There would be no story without them.

Thanks also to Emily Rideout, Katie Itotani, Jeff Henderson, Aiden Axthelm and Anita Bake for being first readers and for giving helpful suggestions. Thanks also to the ladies of ANWA for their inspiration and to Terry Deighton for trying to teach me where to put a comma!

Thanks to my husband Larry for his constant support and encouragement and for the people who said, "write your own story."

Chapter 1

Spring 1948

Vancouver, British Columbia, Canada

Even this early, Jean could already hear the rumble of city traffic. She woke rather reluctantly. She yawned and stretched. Every muscle in her lithe body ached. Yesterday she had spent scrubbing the city grime from every surface of their quaint little home. The new owners would take possession of their one story, wood frame house later that day.

One look towards the window told her it was barely dawn. Allan had said they were leaving at first light, so she had better get cracking. She turned to face him and found him propped up on one elbow, gazing down at her.

"Morning, beautiful!" he greeted her.

"Not hardly."

"What, not morning or not beautiful?"

"Both!" she replied, moaning, "I ache all over!"

"Turn over, and I'll rub your back."

She gratefully accepted a few more minutes to stay in bed. With the stove already loaded on the truck, their house felt cold and a trifle damp. She knew Allan was excited to be leaving behind city life.

"Do you think your Mum will have breakfast ready yet?" he queried.

"I told her we were leaving at first light, so I'm sure she will by the time we get there."

"Well then, I'll roll up the bedding, and you get the boys up."

She rolled out of bed and padded down the hall to the bathroom. She was really going to miss the indoor plumbing. From now on, she would have to make do with a chamber pot and the outdoor biffy. The tin tub was already piled on their functional but rusty 1931 Dodge flat bed truck with all the rest of their belongings. Thank goodness, the radio was right for a change, and it was not raining. It had been the rainiest spring in over a decade. She hoped it would hold off until they unloaded the truck. At least the wooden truck bed had a removable sideboard frame covered with green canvas. Allan would tuck the mattresses and crib under the canvas that morning to help keep them dry, but so far, it appeared to be a clear day.

Jean finished dressing and went across the hall to the boy's room. The expression, "let sleeping dog's lie", came to mind as she gazed with fondness down at the three of them. She wished she could bundle them into the truck without waking them, but she knew that was impossible. They were as excited about the move as their daddy was. She grinned to see Ross in his usual position, tummy down, arms and legs pulled up underneath himself with his bottom sticking up in the air. This had inspired her and Allan's code phrase for the boys being asleep for the night -- bottoms up. Dark haired, sturdy Ross would turn two in just two months.
She crouched down and gently shook the oldest boy, three-year-old Robin. He was tall for his age and thin, with straight brown hair and a smattering of freckles.

"Hey, sleepy head, it's morning."

He popped right up, rubbing his face with the palms of his hands, "Are we going right now, Mummy?"

"Yes, dear."

"Ross, Ross!" he turned and reached across the twin mattress that he shared with his little brother and gave him a rousing shake.

"Come on, Ross. Wake up. We're going to get a puppy and a pony and some cows. We're gonna be cowboys!"

She chuckled, yes they were as excited as their daddy was, maybe more so! Ross woke with a sleepy smile for his momma.

2

She helped them into their clothes she had laid out the night before, all the while answering their chatter, assuring them that yes, they would get there today! Little blonde, curly headed Lanny, barely six months old, was the last one to wake. He had already been up once in the night to feed. She hoped that would hold him until they were underway, so she could nurse him in the truck.

In a manner of minutes, they were all loaded up and bid farewell to the snug little house on 23rd Avenue. Allan had built it for her when Ross was born almost two years ago. He had bought the lot for sixty dollars from the City of Vancouver. He purchased the lumber from an old Air Force barracks for sixty dollars as well. So many happy memories, but she did not look back as Allan pulled the truck out of the drive. He was whistling and grinning ear to ear. The boys were bouncing up and down between them. They were starting a new adventure.

23rd Avenue, Vancouver B.C

Allan was more than glad to give up his job in a local sawmill. He had not owned land he could farm since his father had lost their three-generation Manitoba farm during the depression. She knew it was going to be a challenge. No running water. No electricity. No indoor plumbing. However, she was young, strong, and full of hope.

Allan had worked tirelessly all winter and spring getting the house framed and roofed, and a small pasture and garden area cleared. He hoped to get a barn built before the next fall.

Her father, Charlie Peebles, came to Canada, in 1910 at the age of eighteen, from Broughty Ferry, Scotland. He carried all his worldly belongings in a leather trunk two feet by three feet by five feet. He had worked for a farmer in Saskatchewan with hopes of homesteading. At the age of nineteen, Jean's mother, Jane Blythe Morrison, had also emigrated from Dundee, Scotland to Canada. Boarding the train in Montreal, she came west as far as Saskatchewan to work off her passage with a farmer for a year. She and Charlie met, and in 1913, married, in New Ottawa, Saskatchewan. Charlie's dream of homesteading did not pan out, and times were hard for the small family.

He worked a short time for the government. His job was to go out into the bush country of Northern Saskatchewan to bring in women driven mad by loneliness. He left his own wife and kids alone, in a dirt-floored shack, for weeks at a time. He drove a team of workhorses pulling a wagon that acted as an ambulance. He had told his daughter it sometimes took three men to get one woman into a straight jacket. The women would scream and curse at him all the way to the asylum in North Battleford. Remembering her father's stories, Jean wondered if their farm would be that lonely.

Charlie now worked for the railway, and Jane owned a small store in Vancouver, B.C. Whenever Jane saved up enough money, she would buy land. She had sold Jean and Allan the 18 acres in Mission, where they were now moving, for $200.

They stopped just a few short blocks later on Rupert Street for a hearty breakfast of bacon, eggs, and flapjacks with her folks. Then came the goodbyes and hugs, with a few tears between Jean and her mother, and they got back on the road. It was only about 60 miles away, but the truck only went 25 miles per hour. Today, fully loaded down, it would probably only go 20.

The road followed the Fraser River most of the early part of the trip. It was at flood stage and looked unusually wide and dark. Tree trunks and branches bobbed up and down in the current. When they entered the dense woods, the boys settled down and finally fell asleep. Allan kept up his cheerful whistle, and Jean

4

leaned her head back and closed her eyes. She had better try catching a few winks while the boys were quiet; there was a long day ahead. She had written beforehand to her brother Jack whose property was less than 10 miles from theirs.

"I told Jack we would probably be there by noon. He should be there to help us unload the truck."

Allan barely nodded in reply and continued whistling.

She startled awake when she felt the truck leave the pavement and start on the gravel road. They were getting close. Opening her eyes, she was surprised to see water covering the road. She should have been prepared, with all the talk in the newspapers about the 'Flood of 48.' She looked quickly to Allan.

"It's all right," he assured her quietly. "It's not very deep, and the road is still intact." Allan shifted the truck into low gear, and it shuddered in response. They started up the hill of Nelson Road. The cedars grew thick on both sides of the road interspersed with maples that were already leafing out. She cranked down her window and smelled cedars and damp earth.

At the top of the hill, they passed Ernie Nelson's well-used dairy farm. The acrid odor of cattle wafted through the open window. Jean wrinkled her nose and hurriedly cranked up her window. Allan grinned at her. "It smells like money to me!"

The dairy was acres of green pasture bordered by heavy forest. Mr. Nelson had been running his family farm there since he was 17 years old. He was getting on in years. The boys thought him ancient, but he was still running the dairy. There were other neighbors on the hill, Gabe Masuravich and his wife, Vera and three-year-old daughter, Nina. They farmed the 20 acres adjoining their own. They had met Gabe over the fence line, but they had yet to meet Vera and the little girl. There were also the Bodner's, the Vargas's, Wally and Helen Little, Miss Stewart, and the McNeals.

Jean looked ahead to the bend of the road and could see the little house Allan had built. She looked across at him and smiled. Including her brother's, she did not know anyone who could work as long a day as Allan could.

The road looked like it ended in their front yard, but it made a sharp 90 degree turn and skirting the edge of their property headed on up to yet another hill. On up the second hill lived the Sporie's, Mr. Weatherall, and Chauncey Haight, a Boer War veteran, and his wife, Lillian.

Allan clearing the property with his 1931 Dodge truck set up with a belt off the rear wheel to cut firewood.

They pulled into the yard, and Jean gazed out at their new home. The little four room, tarpapered house stood directly ahead of them in the small yard Allan had first had to clear before building. To one side were the pear tree and two apple trees they had so excitedly planted last fall. She had worried over them surviving the winter, but she could see they were beginning to bud. She had not been out to the farm with Allan in several months and saw that he had cleared a considerable sized pasture.

He pointed to a flat area beyond the house. "I'll start on the barn tomorrow, and we will soon get the boys their cows and a pony!"

She smiled in reply. She had no doubt he would make good on his promise to the boys.

"Come on fellows," she called, opening the door of the truck. "You're at the farm now!" They clambered down and set off, with a whoop, to run about the yard.

The acreage consisted of a large, lush green, flat area where the house, yard, woodshed, and outhouse were located, with room to add the vegetable garden, barn and corral. The corral sloped down to a large, shaded gully. Its gushing Chester Creek would become a summertime delight and life saving source of water for the family. A shallow ravine separated a small hill to the east of the barnyard and a large hill to the north. Cedars, maples, and alders grew thick over all the uncleared portion of the property.

Allan commenced untying the truck's green canvas. Jean set off, toting Lanny up the short staircase to look inside the house. It was no bigger than their home had been in Vancouver, just over 700 square feet, but she was excited just the same. The boys had miles to play in outside; they did not need a big house. Directly opposite the stairs going up were a set of stairs going down to a dirt basement where they would later store their butter, cream, root vegetables, and fruit.

The stairs going up entered directly into a small common room where, to the right, was an open area for their table and chairs and their one upholstered armchair. The house had an unlived in chill about it, but Jean knew they would soon fix that. Allan had built a floor to ceiling cupboard on the wall just inside the door. She saw there was considerable space for her dishes, pots, pans, and canned foods. A counter with a wide porcelain sink sat to the left of the door with room enough for their large wood burning cook stove. The stove would also be their only heat source. Their wooden ice chest would fit the open space on the far wall. Tongue and groove wooden planks covered the floor. She could still smell the fresh aroma of sawdust. Jean would be able to store perishables, in the winter, in a small screened in window box.

"Well, Lanny, let's see if we can find your room, shall we?"

There was a small washroom, empty except for pegs to hang their towels, directly behind the kitchen and then the two bedrooms across the hall from each other. She entered the one on the right.

"I guess you boys will have this one."

She set Lanny down on the floor, and he looked around with interest. He was not crawling yet, and Jean realized with satisfaction that this would be a great advantage today!

"You stay here a minute. Mummy's going to get your things from the truck."

She hurried out to the truck and grabbed his blanket and the cloth bag with the clean diapers. Allan had his arms full of suitcases that he carried in after her.

"Well Jean, what do you think?"

"It's wonderful, Allan! I can't believe all you've gotten done!"

He smiled, pleased at her praise. "Still a lot to get done before winter, but now that we're here full time, I'll be able to work longer days."

She hugged him fiercely, "You'll work yourself to the bone!"

"No other way to be, Jean, if we want to make a go of it. Besides I'd rather die with my boots on."

She gave him a wry grin. "I'll change the baby and then start on some sandwiches for lunch." He went out for another load calling back to her that Jack should be along any minute.

Jean's brother, Jack, arrived with his two boys Johnny, 11 and Stan, 5 before she had finished changing Lanny. The boys were delighted to see their cousins and dragged Stan off to join their exploring while Johnny helped the men unload the truck. Jack's wife, Edna, was due in a matter of weeks with their third child. She would not come today, but she had thoughtfully sent along some cold milk and cookies to add to their noon meal. The men brought the table in first, and while Jean proceeded to get lunch set on it, Johnny packed in the six chairs, one by one, and the high chair. She was happy to get Lanny up off the floor out of harms way and set him in his highchair with a crust of bread to keep him occupied. She called to Allan to bring the crib in next, so she could get it set up for Lanny's nap.

She sent Johnny to the well for a bucket of water. It was located about 50 feet behind the house. Jack had witched the well. He and Jean's other two brothers, Morrie and Bob, had helped Allan dig it out over many weeks. They had gone down 25 feet before they had hit good, clear water in pure sand.

She called the boys to come in to lunch and washed them up at the kitchen sink as best she could with the cold water. It was a merry group at lunch. The boys were so excited with the newness of their surroundings and Allan so happy to share his plans for the place with Jack. He talked of the location and size of the barn, where the corrals and garden would be located.

"What type of cattle do you think would do best here, Jack?"

Allan nodded thoughtfully as Jack replied, but Jean knew he had only asked out of courtesy. Allan was a farmer through and through.

After lunch, the boys went off to climb the hill they had spied beyond the house.

"Johnny, keep an eye on the boys will you?" Jean called after them.

Jean put Lanny down to nap and busied herself with carrying in the boxes of household goods. The men got busy, moving in the heavier items. Luckily, the top and the door came off her heavy cast iron cook stove, or she was afraid just the two men would never have been able to carry it. It was a struggle as it was to get it dragged in place and the chimney flue attached. They brought in the double bed, the boys' twin bed, and their worn burgundy upholstered armchair along with two dressers. They also carried in the heavy wooden icebox. Jean's older sister, Margaret, had given them her old icebox when she bought a fridge. They would not likely be able to run to town whenever it needed ice, but it was a good tight place to store foodstuffs. In a few hours, the truck was unloaded, and some of the wood Allan had cut last fall had been carried in to start a fire before it got dark.

Allan honked the horn on the truck to call the boys in, and Johnny finally brought them back from the woods. Robin was full of plans for the forts they would build and the adventures they would have. Jack was in a hurry to get home to Edna, so he loaded up his boys, and they were off. "See you all real soon."

"Thanks Jack!" Jean and Allan chorused together.

Allan put the large, silver kettle on the stove and soon had warm water to wash up the boys. Jean fetched their pajamas and a towel. Allan lifted them up one by one to bathe them in the big kitchen sink. They would soon have to light the coal oil lamp, as it was already dusk. To save on oil, they would wait as long as possible. Jean got a quick supper, of canned soup and homemade bread on the table, and they ate and laughed at the boy's antics by the soft, flickering light of the lamp.

Jean cuddled the two older boys next to her on the big stuffed armchair to read *The Adventures of Reddy Fox*. Allan walked Lanny up and down the hall, singing to him. Lanny accompanied him with his own sleepy wail, as if he had not the strength left to muster up a full-fledged cry. The boys went down without a fuss, for a change, excited to be in their new home. While Jean nursed Lanny and put him down, Allan heated another kettle to wash up their dishes and make a relaxing cup of tea. Allan washed, and Jean dried and put away. They worked steadily, unpacking and stowing their few belongings. She even convinced Allan to pound a few nails in the wall to hang their mirror and a few treasured pictures. However, they were soon exhausted and fell into bed at last.

"Do you hear that, Jean?"

She listened intently but could only hear the soft occasional popping of the logs in the fire. "What, dear?"

"The quiet."

"Yes," she whispered. "Bottoms up."

Chapter 2

They awoke the next morning to the sound of rain pattering on the roof. The fire had died down during the night and it was chilly in the house. Allan jumped up, added wood to the fire in the stove, and set the kettle on. He came back to their room to dress in woolen socks, rough wool pants over his long woolen underwear and a soft plaid flannel shirt. Over this, he threw his heavy mackinaw and wide brimmed felt hat. "Stay in bed till it warms up Jean. I'll go work a few hours and come back in for breakfast. How did Lanny do?"

"He was only up the once. He'll be up again soon."

"Well, stay in bed as long as you can. I'll be back."

During the night, Allan had thought better of starting first on the barn. A chicken coop would be faster to build, and then they would have their own supply of eggs. He selected a likely spot to the east of the clearing for the barn and corral. He worked steady for several hours before heading back to the house for breakfast. Jean and the boys were up and dressed, and she was feeding them their breakfast of porridge. "Here you are finally! How is our gentleman farmer? Are you soaked thru yet?"

He hung his damp coat and hat on the hooks behind the door. "No, it's just a drizzle. I'm dodging the rain. I decided to build the chicken coop first, so we can have eggs of our own sooner."

"That's great. Speaking of eggs, I thought I would walk over and see if Mrs. Masuravich has any eggs and milk we can buy. The milk Jack brought is almost gone."

"Good idea. I will be going into town later to pick up chicken wire. I'll take the older boys with me."

"Do you boys want to ride into town with your Daddy?" The boys all chorused their approval with baby Lanny not realizing the invitation did not extend to him.

The weather had cleared up after breakfast. Soon after lunch, Allan had the coop roughed in and was ready to take a break to run into town for the chicken wire. Jean dressed the boys to be outside in jackets, boots, and hats. They loved their boots and hated their hats but Jean was adamant. If you wanted to be outside in the winter, spring, or fall, you wore a hat, and there was no arguing on this point. Robin had tried many a time and lost. So, appropriately attired, they were off with Daddy for a trip to town.

Jean meanwhile dressed Lanny to go and meet their nearest neighbors for the first time. She hoped Vera would be a little more approachable than her husband, Gabe, had been. He had been quite abrupt the day they had met him over the adjoining fence line, but perhaps, she thought charitably, he was just uncomfortable speaking English. It was a short walk, and the air was scrubbed clean after the morning of rain. She could hear water dripping off the trees that bordered the road. The birds sounded as happy with the sunshine as she was. She was glad they had waited until late spring to make this move. The driveway to the Masuravich's ran straight along the edge of their property, going directly past the house to a long low chicken barn. She could hear the chickens cackling like gossipy old women, and wrinkling her nose, she thought for the first time how glad she was that Allan had built their chicken coop a little farther from the house. With Lanny slung over her hip, Jean walked the grassy hump down the center of the driveway, avoiding the mud puddles. The Mausuravich's house was low and narrow; it seemed built to leave the maximum amount of space for cattle. Like Jean and Allan's, it was unpainted. She approached the wood slat door and knocked. She noticed the door closed with a latch, not a doorknob. A short, solid woman opened the door a crack and peered out.

"Hello, my name is Jean Irwin. We have moved into our house just up the road from you."

Jean tried a friendly smile. The door swung open wide.

"Aaah! Yah! You come in. You set down. You haf some coffee."

Vera immediately served a strong, black, cup of coffee to Jean and began to fuss over Lanny.

"Such a beautiful baby! Such beautiful curls! She is a girl, Yah?"

Jean laughed; she was used to the question. Lanny's curly blonde hair and big blue eyes with long lashes made him a very pretty baby for a boy. "No, this is a beautiful boy!"

Lanny- 1948

They visited a half an hour or so and agreed on a price for eggs and milk. Vera told her they had left Eastern Europe just before the war and had settled here in Mission. Jean finally left with the eggs, but Vera insisted her husband, Gabe, would bring over the milk that night after the milking.

"You are too little a thing to carry your baby and a big jug of milk. I will haf Gabe save you out a gallon every day till you haf your own cows."

Jean thanked her and headed home, relieved and delighted with her friendly neighbor.

The boys were excited to be off on an errand with their daddy. Robin could see out the window of the truck, but Ross's head did not clear the top of the dash. Robin described the passing scenery to Ross.

"There is a big barn and cows, Ross, but not any horses. I don't think a cowboy lives here." This he declared as they passed Mr. Nelson's dairy at the top of the hill. "Now we are coming down a huge hill, and we are going to fall right into a lake!" A little shriek accompanied this last part of his boyish chatter. Allan stopped the truck and set the emergency brake.

"Now, boys," he said as he lifted Ross up, so he could see out, "the river has flooded over the road, but the water is not deep, and we will drive very slowly through it and will be safe. Alright?"

The boys made no reply but continued to stare out the window. Ross' little mouth opened in an "oh," but no sound came out. Allan set Ross back down on the seat, released the brake and, putting the truck in gear, crept slowly forward.

"Look, Robin, how you can see where the road is through the water?"

His nose pressed against the side window, Robin made no reply. Ross curled up in a ball on the seat of the truck. He began a little whimper. The truck crept forward, and the water sprayed noisily on the underside of the truck. They were soon on dry ground again. Robin continued his cheerful prater. Allan began to whistle a tune, and Ross sat up again to watch the dash of the truck.

Allan pointed out a train going slowly along next to the flooded Fraser pushing up a wave of muddy water with its cowcatcher.

"See that, Robin? Now remember, in this country don't buy land where something can wash over it or where something can fall on top of it or where it can slide off the edge of something. Because in this country, if it can happen, it *will* happen. Many people down here on the flats lost a great deal of livestock this year, and some of them their homes as well. You be sure and build on high ground."

The small town of Mission was just 4 miles up the highway. Allan made a quick stop at Horvath's gas station at the corner of 7th Avenue and Hurd Road and asked the attendant for a dollar's worth of fuel. While the man pumped the gas and washed the window, Allan took a dollar bill from his wallet folded it carefully in half, so it looked like two one-dollar bills and, handing it out the window, said to the attendant, "Keep the change!" He chuckled about that all the way to Buckerfield's Feed Store.

He took the boys in to buy the chicken wire and some feed. He was counting on Gabe selling him some poultry tomorrow.

"Now you boys can look all you want but don't touch anything!"

The boys meandered through a wonderland of painted farm equipment all enveloped with the wonderful thick odor of numerous grains. Allan picked out a 30-foot roll of chicken wire and a 50-pound bag of feed. The clerk told him to drive his truck around back, and he would load the feed on for him. The two boys reluctantly left the store with their Daddy and climbed back up into the truck. Allan drove around to the loading dock. He lifted Ross to look through the back window while the bag of grain was loaded. It made a dusty thump on the bed of the truck, and the boys gave a little holler of approval.

Allan started up the old truck and wheeled out onto the back street of Mission.

"Let's take this street out of town, shall we boys?"

Robin again began to give Ross a travelogue.

"There's a train station but no train."

At this, Ross struggled to stand, but Allan pushed him down again. After another block, Allan pulled the truck over to the curb and came to a stop. He had spied a hardware store and decided to purchase some more nails while he was in town.

Setting the emergency brake he said, "You boys wait here. I will be right back."

Allan entered the store and approached the counter where a middle-aged man with a nametag that read Carl Anderson, Manager greeted him. "Can I help you?"

"Yes, I want to buy a box of nails."

"Sure, let me show you what we have. I've not seen you in here before. Are you new in town?"

"Yep. My names Allan Irwin. I have a place up on Nelson Road."

"Irwin? Are you the guy who blew apart the old Catholic Church at Durieu?"

"Yep, that was me."

Allan chuckled to remember the reaction of the neighbors of the church in Durieu. He had stopped at all the nearby homes to let them know he would be setting off the dynamite as part of his salvage operation, and everyone's response was the same.

"If you set off dynamite there won't be anything left to build with!"

He had proven them wrong and had taken a board from the roof of the church, to the Fraser Valley Record, signed by the builder: J.E Moorhouse, Hatzic Prairie B.C. May 22, 1865. There had been some disagreement about the date. Many of the local residents thought the church had not been built until 1885. The newspaper had published a picture of the old church and an article on the demolition.

The church at Durieu.

"Yeah," Anderson continued, "Jack Heptonstall was in here last fall, telling me about you hanging a stick of dynamite from the rafters to loosen up all the nails in the building. He thought you were going to blow that church to kingdom come!"

"Yep, got all the wood and windows for my house and barn out of that old church."

"Well, I never did hear tell of using dynamite for such a thing before!" exclaimed Anderson.

The boys were climbing all over the inside of the truck by this time. Robin had taken up residence at the driver's wheel, yanking it side to side, making rumbling truck noises, and loud beeps. Ross had climbed up to stand, without daddy there to keep him pushed down, and was peering through the rear window behind the seat. It was more a rough-cut opening, than a window, in the timbers that formed the back of the cab. He tried to stick his head out but could not manage to. He turned his head sideways and was just able to get it through the window. About this time, Robin noticed what Ross was up to and climbing up to stand beside him, yelled, "Ross, you better get back in here!"

Ross obediently tried to comply, as he had not the view he had first imagined, but found he could not get his head back through the window. On this discovery, he started to wail, and Robin, being ever so helpful, started to pull. This proved so uncomfortable for Ross that he set off screaming at the top of his lungs. Robin meanwhile kept yelling, "Ross, you stop that and get in here!" Several people had gathered around to watch this interesting spectacle by the time Allan came back out of the hardware store with the box of nails in arm. He could not see what was going on at the truck for the people gathered around it, but he could tell by the screaming and hollering that something was amiss. He deposited the box on the back of the truck; next to the huge sack of grain and looked up to see Ross's little head stuck in the truck's rear window. Hopping up on the flat bed, he hushed Ross and, with some mild irritation, instructed Robin to stop pulling. Then, gently turning Ross's head to the side, he gave it a little push, and Ross tumbled back through the window and onto the seat. Allan waded through the relieved audience and hopped into the truck.

"It's a good thing your Mother was not here. She would have been mortified."

Allan chuckled all the way home.

Jean carried Lanny out to meet the truck when they pulled into the yard.

"Did you boys behave yourselves in town today?"

"I must say your boys made quite an impression in town," Allan answered.

"That's good," Jean, said. "Handsome is as handsome does."

Allan looked at Robin and winked.

Chapter 3

Allan arranged with Gabe Masuravich for the purchase of ten chickens. Gabe even had wooden crates Allan could borrow to carry them home. By late the next morning, the coop and run were finished. Allan, Robin, and Ross set off after lunch in the truck, to bring the chickens' home. They drove down the Masuravich's bumpy driveway, the boys bouncing on the seat, past the house to the chicken barn. The boys had never seen so many chickens. They wrinkled their noses at the nasty stench. "They're kind of ugly. Aren't they, Daddy?"

"Yes, Robin. There's not a bird uglier or dumber than a chicken, but they sure taste good!"

The boys laughed to watch daddy and the gruff Mr. Masuravich try to catch the frantic birds. Feathers flew, and the birds squawked like crazy. Robin thought to himself, that even though the birds were dumb, they were smart enough to keep away from daddy. Finally, they had ten birds crated up. Allan paid Gabe, thanked him for his help, and they were on their way home. Everyone was in good spirits; their farm was starting to take shape.

Allan worked on fencing all the next week, and by the following Saturday, had a large enough pasture to go to auction and bring home two milk cows. He had dug a portion of the bank on the small hill away, so he could back the truck up to it and off load the cows directly to the hill. Jean and the boys came out to watch this operation with great interest. Allan untied the cows from the wooden frame he had built around the truck bed. They were a brown- eyed golden Jersey and dark brown, black- faced Guernsey. He led them down the hill to the pasture.

"Well, boys, here are your cows! What do you think you should name them?"

Robin had apparently given this some thought already and, pointing to the light colored Jersey, shouted, "Daisy!"

"A great name for a cow! What about the other one?"

Robin shrugged his shoulders, "I dunno."

Jean thought a minute and then said, "I like the name Bessie."

"Bessie it is!" Allan agreed. They had a start on their herd.

Bessie

Jean had spent the morning baking bread, and the warm yeasty smell permeated the small house.

"Nothing like the smell of baked bread, eh boys?" remarked Allan.

They had just sat down to bread and honey when Jack drove in the yard with Stan.

"Hello, Jack! Come in and have a bite."

"Thanks, but I can't stay. I just dropped Edna off at the hospital. The baby's on its way! I stopped in town to phone

Mom. Dad is bringing her out on the train to stay for a few weeks. Do you think you could pick them up at the station tomorrow morning, Allan? Johnny is at school, but can you keep Stan today, Jean?"

"Of course! You and Johnny come by for dinner tonight."

"That will be great, Jean, thanks."

While Jack hurried back to town, Stan joined them at the table and excitedly told the boys what they might name their new baby. "We might call him Charlie, or Robert, or maybe Frank."

Jean asked, "What will you name it if it's a girl?"

"A girl!" Stan snorted. "It's not going to *be* a girl!"

"Maybe you could name it Bessie if it is," Robin offered gallantly.

Jean took the boys all out for a walk to the gully after clearing lunch away. Through the cow pasture, past a grazing Daisy and Bessie, who chewing rhythmically, glanced at them with huge, mournful eyes. Up and over the big hill they went with the three boys trotting to keep up.

The gully was an amazing place for little boys to play. It had huge, lush green Boston ferns and a smaller lacey fern with a black stem that Jean loved. Giant cedar trees and the rushing, rock filled stream provided cool, damp shade. She would not let them down there yet by themselves, but she would often accompany them and even let them throw rocks into the creek. This they could do by the hour. Today she sat with Lanny on her lap while the boys played.

"Come on, fellows, time for Mummy to get back and start dinner. You boys can show Stan your fort on the hill."

The smaller of the two hills was directly behind the chicken coop. It was also the closest to the house, and Jean would let them play there all by themselves as long as they answered when she called to them. They had built a fort by dragging small logs and fallen branches to form walls. Some days it was a castle, some days a boat. Some days it was an Army fort that Indians attacked. They had asked Jean to tie one of her rags to a stick for a flag. Tall trees sheltered their fortress, they could even play out there in the rain and not get very wet at all.

Allan had a good start on the barn, and Jean sent Robin out to drag him in for dinner when Jack and Johnny arrived. "Well Jack, do you have any news?"

"It's a girl!" Johnny blurted out.

"A girl!" Stan repeated in disgust.

"Now Stan," Jean encouraged, "a girl can be a good thing. Now you will have a Maid Marion when you play Robin Hood, a Wendy when you play Peter Pan and a Princess to rescue when you play Knights and Castles." Stan did not look convinced.

"Have you picked out a name yet, Jack?"

"Yes, Edna wants to call her Shirley," Jack said smiling.

"What a sweet name," Jean responded. "I can't wait to meet her!"

Jack had brought a small bag of clothes, so Stan could stay over night, and as Jean helped the boys dress for bed that night, Stan asked in earnest, "Auntie Jean, maybe I could come live with you?"

"Don't you think you would miss your Mommy and Daddy, Stanley?"

Stan made no reply and went to bed that night with a frown still furrowing his brow.

As Jean drifted off to sleep that night, she offered a prayer of gratitude that Edna and Shirley were healthy. "And Lord, if you don't mind, could I have a daughter someday, too?"

Allan picked up Grandma and Granddad Peebles at the station the next morning. Like many of their contemporaries, they did not own a car. Allan brought them over to the farm before taking them on to Jack's place. Jean and Allan were pleased to be able to show them around and proud of the progress they had made. Grandma had brought several jars of her home canned peaches that Jean was thrilled to receive. Granddad helped Allan with work on the barn while Jean and Grandma chatted, and Grandma fussed over the boys.

Grandma thought, by early afternoon, they should be off in order to meet Johnny when he came in from school. Jean promised they would be over soon to visit, at least by the time Edna came home from the hospital at the end of her week. Granddad said he would come back and help with the barn.

He and Jack both came back the next several evenings after they finished the chores at Jack's place to work on the barn. By the end of the week, it was finished and Allan proudly showed Jean the completed project. It was a simple structure, roughly built, designed to hold just four cows. A manger ran along the front of the stalls. There was a small hayloft overhead. Allan planned to add a decent sized hayloft in the winter when he had more time. He needed to start getting the garden dug. Jack had brought over a gunnysack of seed potatoes, and Allan asked Jean to make up a list of what else she might want.

Every day that followed, Allan was out digging over the area he had marked off to be their garden. He would dig shovelfuls of virgin earth, break it up with the hoe, and then finally rake it to break it down in size as much as possible. It was tough work. Jean helped with the rake or the hoe as much as possible, but it was heavy work for her light frame. Allan would shoo her off whenever she began to look tired. After a week of this, he declared at dinner one night that Gabe had told him all danger of a frost was past, and so they were all to help the next day to get their garden planted.

"Can we help Daddy?"

"Of course, Robin. It will be your job to plant the seeds."

The next morning Jean carried an old quilt out to the edge of the garden lot and set Lanny on it with a metal pot and a big serving spoon. It was his favorite 'toy' at the moment. Allan pounded two wooden stakes in the newly turned earth, tied a string to both to mark a straight row, and began to hoe down the length of the garden. Jean showed the boys how to drop the tiny seeds one by one into the rows Allan made. She followed along behind covering up the seeds. Planted in less than two hours, their garden contained peas, carrots, beets, potatoes, onions, broccoli, beans, cabbages, tomatoes, and cauliflower. Jean imagined she would have to eat the cauliflower all by herself; even Allan refused to touch it. It was wonderful to look out at their finished garden and know they would have food to eat through the winter.

Allan declared they had all worked so hard that tomorrow would be a holiday, and they would go over to see Grandma Peebles and Edna's new baby at Uncle Jack's. The boys cheered at the thought of getting to play with their cousins. Jean had crocheted a lovely pink blanket to take to baby Shirley. She had also made herself a new dress of pink, white, and blue checks. It was the first dress she had ever sewn, and she was immensely proud of it and excited at the chance to wear it.

The next afternoon, with all the chores done, Allan loaded the boys into the truck while Jean went to change. She came out the front door in her new dress with Shirley's blanket wrapped in white tissue paper. Robin turned to Allan and said, "She looks just like a little girl, doesn't she Daddy?"

Chapter 4

Robin was the first to notice there was something going on between Mommy and Daddy. There was a lot of whispering, and then they would stop talking when either he or Ross came near. After two or three days of this odd behavior, Jean said one night as she tucked them in, one on either end of their shared twin bed, "do you know what tomorrow is boys?" They shook their heads no.

"It is Ross's birthday! You will be two years old, Ross!" She showed him how to hold up two fingers.

Robin had just one question. "Are we going to have cake?"

Allan had been hard at work everyday fencing, but he stayed inside next morning until the boys were up in honor of Ross's birthday. They had applesauce pancakes for breakfast, which was Ross's favorite, mostly because of the delectable maple syrup, and then Jean announced that there was a little present outside for Ross.

"Would you like to go out and see?" The boys rushed to the front door but saw nothing outside. "That's funny," Jean said, "maybe you should try the back door."

They ran down the hall and struggled to throw open the back door. There, just beyond the porch in the back yard, to the side of the woodshed, they saw a brand new red wagon. They were busy the rest of the day towing each other and pretending it was a boat or a car or a covered wagon. They only came in when Jean called them for lunch and Robin remembered about the cake.

Robin and Ross plowing with the wagon.

"Come on Ross! There's going to be cake!"

Jean had spent most of the morning cutting out marshmallows in the shape of bunny heads that decorated the outside edge of Ross's round birthday cake, which was dusted with green coconut. The boys thought it was the most delicious looking thing they had ever seen. She let them have a small slice after lunch, but she made them save the rest until Jack's family came over later that night.

Ross with his bunny birthday cake.

That evening they lit a bon fire outside from Allan's brush clearing and carried out the kitchen chairs for the adults. Johnny tirelessly pulled the boys round and round the yard in the wagon.

All the adults took a turn to hold little Shirley. She was a beautiful baby. Jean told Edna she was lucky to have a girl. "I don't think my Stan would agree with you, Jean!" Edna chuckled.

Johnny and Stan brought Ross a gift of toy cowboys and Indians all on little brown horses. Ross thought it grand to have a birthday, if only every day could be this much fun!

Several days later, Jean put Lanny down for a nap. She shooed Ross and Robin outdoors to play for the afternoon and on hands and knees set out to wash the floors in the living area.

"Mummy, Mummy," Robin called through the window only twenty minutes later, "the sky is falling!"

"What?"

"The sky is falling!"

Just two nights ago, Jean had told the boys the story of Henny Penny.

She sighed, "Now Robin," she shouted, "you're not supposed to tell tales!"

Just then, she heard a distant rumble. Jumping to her feet she threw open the front door. The boys were standing in the yard staring up at a lowering black sky. A gust of moisture-laden wind rushed toward her.

"Inside!" she commanded.

She waited to see Robin grab Ross by the arm and begin to haul him toward the house. Then she hurried through the back door, grabbed her coat from its hook, and headed outside calling for Allan. She heard him shout back and then saw him stick his head out the barn door.

"I've got the cattle in Jean! I'll come to the house in a minute!"

The wind was picking up as she turned and raced back to the house. She heard another deep rumble but closer this time. Helping the boys off with their sweaters, she stood them before the front window. It was low enough that they could see out. They gripped the ledge with their fingers and pressed their tiny noses against the glass.

"You might see some lightening."

"What's lightening, Mummy?"

"You'll see." She struggled to shut the front door against the wind.

She heard Allan come in the back. "Looks like it will be a real gully washer! I tethered the cows in their stalls, so they wouldn't thrash around if it gets too noisy."

They heard a tremendous crack directly overhead, and the boys shouted and pointed. "We saw it!" Thunder rumbled, and the boys jumped up and down and clapped their little hands. The clouds opened up, and the rain began to pour down, thundering on the roof and slashing against the windows. Jean sighed and put away her bucket; the floors would have to wait for another day.

While the boys watched for more lightening, Jean busied herself making up a large pot of vegetable beef soup. Allan helped her chop the vegetables.

"Nothing better to eat on a stormy day than soup, Jean."

The storm eventually rumbled past, but the rains continued to hammer their little house. Allan paced, and, now that the thunder and lightning show was over, the boys were starting to get restless as well. Jean suggested Allan might get his fiddle out.

Allan and his next oldest sister, Grace, had spent their youth, in the long prairie winter months, playing for country dances. Grace played the piano while Allan played the fiddle. He had not had it out since their move to the farm. Standing on a kitchen chair, he retrieved it from the safety of the top shelf of the cupboard, dusted off its amber finish and rosined up the bow. Jean heard Lanny waking up from his nap. She changed him and set him close to his Daddy in the high chair. While Allan played many a merry jig, and Jean took up her never-ending mending, the boys danced around the table, and little Lanny pounded his hands on his tray to the music.

The rain had finally slowed to a trickle when Allan ran out to the barn to do the milking in the late afternoon. It was wonderful to have milk from their cows. Besides the milk, they had all the cream and butter they could possibly use. The creamer sat inside a tin basin filled with cold well water on top of the icebox. It was a tall steel container with a handle topped lid and a glass slotted window that allowed Jean to see when the milk and cream had separated. Drained out through a tap at the base of the creamer, the milk stayed at room temperature for drinking. The cream was drained into a separate pitcher and used, most often for butter, or, on special occasions, for whipping cream.

The cattle looked as though they had come through the storm without any harm.

"Well, our barn stood up to the storm, Jean. There are branches down all over the yard and a few shingles missing. You boys can help pick those up tomorrow and we will have enough for another bonfire. I'll get up on the roof and get it patched in the morning."

That night they fell asleep to the soft patter of rain from a spent storm on the roof.

Chapter 5

Jean hummed as she washed up the breakfast dishes and watched the boys play in the yard with their wagon. She and Allan both agreed it had been the best present ever!

"Boys love things that go!" he had assured her when they had discussed what to get Ross for his second birthday. Both boys had certainly been going ever since.

Today was June 21, 1948, Jean and Allan's fifth anniversary. She did not think he had remembered and she hoped to surprise him with his favorite chocolate cake. She thought back to the night they had first met, December 6, 1942. It was the Heather Concert and Ball, and many of the servicemen stationed in Vancouver were there. Allan was a Corporal in the Royal Canadian Air Force assigned to Sea Island and looked good in his uniform. He was five foot ten with dark hair and 'prairie blue eyes'.

1943

Jean was a pretty girl, five foot six, with a slender build, light brown hair, and blue eyes with long lashes. For Allan it was love at first sight. Jean had needed a little convincing. However, she noticed that he was not drinking as some of his buddies were, and that impressed her. He also kept her laughing most of the night; she smiled to herself now as she thought of it. She had not been interested enough to even tell him her name, but considered him a 'very good dancer.' Her sisters, Margaret and Mary, got into the act and told him her name was Genevieve. He had asked for her phone number at the end of the evening, but she had not thought it proper to give it to him. As she and her sisters were leaving the dance with Margaret's husband, Tony, Margaret inquired of Jean if Allan had asked for her number. When she replied that he had asked, but she had not given it to him, Margaret ran back into the dance and gave him the family's phone number.

Several days later, he phoned when Jean happened to be out. He told her mother he had a '48'. She, not understanding the military lingo for a 48-hour leave, relayed the message to Jean.

"I suppose he wants you to go help him drink it."

It was not long before Jean and Allan were seeing each other every chance they could get. Jean's family liked the man from Manitoba, but she was only twenty-three, and Allan, eighteen years her senior, was forty-one.

Allan had been to a dance without Jean, and had won the fifty-dollar door prize. He wanted to buy her an engagement ring. Having already been twice engaged, Jean wanted no more engagements and impulsively said, "Wait awhile, and maybe you can buy two rings at once." Encouraged, he immediately went out and bought a matched set, engagement ring and wedding band.

They had only known each other six months, and Jean's mother, characteristically speaking her mind, said, "You're taking an awful chance, Jean, marrying someone you know so little about."

Allan replied, "Well, I'm taking the same chance!"

Jean had shyly smiled her approval, but her mother gave him a severe glare.

Allan's Air Force buddy, Jack Mellis, told him he was crazy. "She'll never stay with you, a young girl like that."

The only encouraging person was Jean's sister, Margaret, who said, "Allan is my ideal of the kind of man every girl should marry."

Allan was easy going and hardworking. They made a happy couple and set the date for June 15. However, fate intervened.

Jean had been having abdominal pain, and since the family had a strong history of appendicitis, the family doctor, Dr. R.G. Weldon, decided to do exploratory surgery. It was an infected appendix, and the doctor removed it.

Meanwhile, Allan had been suffering with a severe sore throat. His pal Jack had an atomizer with medication he thought highly effective and suggested Allan use it. Allan spent the next fifteen days in the hospital, lost 30 pounds, and came close to dying from a severe reaction to the atomizer.

They were finally married June 21 out of her parent's home at 3980 Rupert Street at 7pm on a Monday evening by the Air

Force padre. Allan brought Jack Mellis, to stand as best man. Jean's attendants were her little sister, Ruth, and her niece, Carole, Margaret and Tony's daughter.

Jean's bridal gown was a long blue party dress with puffed sleeves and a smocked bodice. In her hair, she wore a hair band of matching blue flowers. She wore a corsage of white gardenias and red roses. Around her neck, she proudly wore the heart shaped necklace, displaying the Air Force insignia, which Allan had made in a shop on base while recovering from his illness. He wore his Air Force uniform.

Allan and Jean June 21, 1943.

Her present to him was a leather autograph album. On the first page she wrote,

"Sweetheart, I thought you would like to know

That someone's thoughts go where you go.

That someone never can forget

The hours we have spent since first, we met.

Remember? Jean."

Jean's mother fixed a lovely dinner. Allan sang an old ballad. "Oh the faces I see don't appeal to me, for it's your face I long for the while, though the hours seem long and the days go wrong, for it's empty with you away. I dream of your lips, your eyes so blue, and I wonder if your heart is dreaming too. I'm lonely for you."

Their honeymoon was a 1200-mile train trip to Russell, Manitoba to spend ten days with Allan's family. Allan whistled all the way. She recalled how nervous she had been about meeting his father Joseph, his two older sisters, Bella and Grace, and Bella's husband, Mac. His mother, Jess, had passed away when Allan was only thirteen years old.

All fear of meeting them soon dissipated as they welcomed her warmly. They told her they had given up all hope of Allan ever marrying and said she had saved him from becoming a confirmed old bachelor. She found Joseph delightful. He was soft spoken, short, and rosy with twinkling Irish blue eyes and a huge drooping mustache.

It was to be the first and last time she was to see the kindly old gentleman as he passed on just two weeks after Robin was born the following year. They happily named little Robin, Robin Joseph after his grandfather.

She found a dear and lasting friend in Grace who was one of the most talented and energetic women she had ever met. Grace could do almost anything. She had taken over the household, when she was eighteen, on the death of her mother, had raised Allan while Bella, "worked out" at a bank (the first female teller in Hamiota, Manitoba), and had cared for her father for the last thirty years. She could sew anything, her gift to Allan and Jean had been a beautiful blue satin, quilted double comforter filled with hand-carded wool from her south neighbor. She could wield a wide assortment of tools. She and Jean would be faithful letter writers for the next thirty-seven years.

Jean smiled to herself, "No," she had no regrets. Jean waited until Allan had come in for lunch and gone out again before she started on the cake. She hoped the darn oven would bake it evenly! She chuckled to herself. He was so busy working the farm he had forgotten their anniversary, she was sure. She felt just the tiniest bit guilty for having hidden away the cards from her parents, Bella, and Grace, but there were so few surprises. She wanted to take advantage of this one.

"My, this looks good!" he exclaimed when she served up roast beef and mashed potatoes and gravy at dinner. She just smiled. When she brought out the cake, the boys whooped their approval.

"Is it my birthday, Mummy?" Robin asked.

"No dear, its Mummy and Daddies' anniversary!"

Out of the corner of her eye, she saw Allan stop with his fork in mid-rise.

"Yes," he responded quickly, "and in honor of the occasion, we'll be holding a dance right after dinner

She grinned at him, and he winked back. Yes, she had surprised him but she would never let him know that she knew it. Dinner was a great success, especially the chocolate cake, and they enjoyed, afterwards, opening the cards family had sent. His sister Grace's card contained an interesting announcement. She was bringing over a gentleman friend from Crescent Beach, where she had moved after the death of her father, to meet them the following Sunday!

"Oh Allan! Wouldn't it be wonderful if Grace were to marry?"

Grace at this time was forty-nine years of age. Bella had married at age thirty-nine and Allan at forty-two, so the siblings had a tradition of late marriages. Grace had always asserted it was because the Irwin's were "the ugliest people on the face of the earth."

Allan pushed the table and chairs up to the wall, got down his fiddle, and played and played while the boys skipped, and Jean danced about the room with Lanny.

The following Sunday, Grace arrived with her gentleman friend, Walter McKibben. Grace was deaf as a fence post and wore a large hearing aid on a ribbon around her neck that she kept tucked in the bodice of her dress. It gave her the appearance of having three bosoms, only the middle one was rectangular.

Grace, Jean holding Lanny and Ross, Robin, Allan Bella.

Luckily, the weather on Sunday was balmy, and so they were able to show the visitors around the farm. The boys introduced them to Daisy and Bessie and then took them to see the chickens.

"And what did you name the chickens?" Auntie Grace loudly asked Robin and Ross.

"Awe, Auntie Grace, you don't give something as ugly as a chicken a name!" Robin shouted to her. The adults did not have an argument for that.

They were impressed with the huge vegetable garden. Grace promised to come in the fall and help Jean do the canning. "I don't know how you will manage it, Jean, with all these babies about." Grace said.

Robin looked around and thought to himself, *"We only have the one baby!"*

However, he thought it best not to contradict his Auntie Grace. Mummy was very particular about what he said to company. It might have been pushing it to call the chickens ugly earlier, even though he knew Daddy agreed with it.

Mummy was proud of the chickens. She had shown him how to reach under them carefully and feel through the prickly hay for the chalky white eggs. She had also told him quite severely that he must not chase them or frighten them, or they would not lay for the family. He knew eggs were one of the things Mummy put in her cakes. He guessed that was why the chickens were so important to her.

Auntie Grace had brought shiny silver toy guns with black holsters for Robin and Ross, and a brown, stuffed teddy bear for Lanny. Jean thanked her but mildly chided her, "You will spoil them Grace!"

"Nonsense," said Grace.

When the boys were running about with their toy guns getting under foot, Allan lost all patience and yelled at them.

Grace said, "You were much worse when you were a child!"

It was the first time the boys ever considered their Dad had actually been a child.

Jean had fixed a lovely meal and it turned out to be a great visit. Walter even donned a pair of Allan's work boots and helped with the evening chores. At dusk, Grace and Walter set off, and the family stood by the road and waved.

"It's so nice to have some of your family nearby, Allan. What did you think of Walter?"

"He's a nice enough chap. I hope she marries him."

"Then I will write and tell her you said so!"

"She'll hardly be worried about what I think."

"Of course she is, Allan. That's why she brought him here. She wants to know if we approve of him."

They gave the boys another half hour to run and play outdoors. They ran about the yard making "pew, pew" noises for their guns. The extra daylight in the summer months was heaven for the boys. It was hard to stick to their bedtimes when it was still light out. However, Jean and Allan were both of the consensus that if they wore them out by playing longer outdoors, they would go to sleep all the faster when they finally got them in to bed.

At least the toy guns had kept Robin on the ground today. He was just learning to climb the trees. Ross would stand watching him and warn him if he thought Robin was getting too high. However, Robin had no fear of heights and would get as high as the branches within reach would let him. Jean would complain bitterly about the sticky pitch on his hands from the cedar tree bark. It was hard to scrub off.

When the boys were finally in bed, Jean asked Allan what he thought they should do for Robin's birthday.

"It might be a good time to get that dog I promised them."

"Have you any idea where we could get one?"

"I'll ask at Buckerfield's Feed next time I'm in town. He'll probably have heard if someone has pups to give away."

Chapter 6

Allan purchased three other cows, and their abundant milk supply was the family's total income. One day at noon, when Allan came in for lunch, he approached Jean about a conversation he had that morning with Mike Zawada. Mike drove the milk route and picked up their milk once a day.

"He wants to know if I need a job. He has another route he is opening, and he said I could drive this one."

"Allan, would you be able to take care of the cattle here and do that also?"

"I think so Jean. If you can take sole charge of the garden, I will be able to do the milking and the route."

She looked at him with concern. She knew he had no thought for himself. It was only about her and the children in his mind. He had an enormous sense of responsibility for their wellbeing.

"The boys are growing up fast, Jean. They are going to need shoes and coats, and we are going to have to have more income to provide for them than what we can make on this farm. I can clear more land, but we still would not be able to handle that many more cattle on our own here."

"All right dear. I'm sure you are right."

"I'll talk to Mike in the morning."

Allan watched for Mike's truck next morning, and when he saw it stop at Gabe's, he hurried down to his own stand. The milk stands were a platform beside the road built the same height as the back of the milk truck. The farmers had to wrestle their

100-pound milk cans up on top of the platform, so the driver could pull right alongside to load the cans and drop off more cans for the next milking. Most of the small farmers had built handcarts, as had Allan, to haul the heavy cans from the barn to the milk stand.

Lanny in the milk cart

"Morning, Allan!"

"Morning, Mike. The Missus and I discussed the job, and if you still have it open, I'd like to take it."

"Great, glad to hear it. Can you meet me at my house tomorrow at six, and I will drive you over the route?"

Allan did some quick calculations in his mind. In order to have his five cows milked and be to Mike's on time, he would have to be up by 4am. "No problem. I'll be there."

"Thanks Allan."

Mike shook his hand and was on his way. Allan hurried off to give the garden a good hoeing and get some more firewood cut.

Thus began Allan's career as a milk truck driver. He was up every day at four to milk the cows, and then he walked the three miles through the brush and woods to Mike's to pick up the truck. The route ended up back at Mike's where he set off to walk back the three miles home, arriving about two-thirty in the afternoon. Each evening there would be another milking, which they would keep for their own use. They had all the milk, butter, cream, and also eggs from their chickens they could possibly eat.

It was on the milk route that Allan saw the sign. Free Puppies. For the next several days, he watched the yard with the sign, and on the third day, he saw the farmer headed across the yard to his barn. He honked the horn, and the farmer veered over to the milk stand.

"Hey, will you save me one of your pups until the seventeenth of this month? I've got a boy with a birthday coming up."

"Sure, no problem!"

Allan whispered the news to Jean later that night. She was delighted. "He is going to be so excited!"

The sign had also given Allan an idea. In a few days, he hammered a sign of his own to his milk stand. It read, 'Wood for Sale'. Allan would continuously cut and haul firewood for the next twenty-five years, greatly augmenting the family income.

Allan picked up the pup on July 17th and kept him in a wooden box on the floor of the truck for the duration of the milk route.

He then carried him home through the bush and shut him up in the barn overnight. He and Jean snuck out to see him with a flashlight and a bowl of milk after the boys were asleep. He was a lovely puppy, brown with golden markings and a good nature about him.

Jean knelt down and ruffled the fur around his ears. "He should do well with the boys!"

"Yes!" Allan laughed. "If he survives them!"

Jean laughed.

They made him a clean bed of hay, plopped him down, and hoped he would sleep through the night. Luckily, he was used to barn living, and they did not hear any yapping or howling out of him.

The next morning Allan got up at four as usual to do the milking, leaving the pup a brimming bowl of milk and shutting the door to the barn. When he drove the milk truck up to his own place, he parked it after loading the cans and hustled over to the barn. Cuddling the puppy, he carried him to the house and, leaving him on the porch, entered the back door.

"Is there a boy with a birthday here?" He called out.

Robin and Ross both came running. Allan picked up Ross, and tousling Robin's hair, said, "Four years old today. I think it's a birthday you'll always remember!"

Jean came with Lanny in her arms and shot Allan a questioning look. He motioned his head towards the back porch. "Open the door, Robin."

Robin struggled with two hands to turn the knob but finally got it open. There on the back porch was a small, stinky brown pile of dog droppings. Robin turned and gave his parents a look that clearly said, "What a cruel present to give a little kid!"

"Oh, oh!" said Jean.

Allan laughed, "There must be a puppy in here somewhere!"

Sure enough with a little coaxing, the puppy emerged from under Jean's wringer washer. All the boys squealed with delight! Jean thrust Allan his lunch pail, and he was off with a mad dash to the truck to make up for lost time. The boys spent the day happily playing with Sparky, as Robin named him. Robin had even forgotten about birthday cake until after dinner. The boys were very concerned about Sparky spending the night alone. Only with continual reassurances, were they finally able to shut him in the barn and come in for bed.

Ross, Sparky, Robin.

The summer days were full of play for the three boys and full of hard work for Jean and Allan. Every spare minute for Jean, when she was not baking, cleaning, or washing clothes in her gas powered wringer washer, was spent to tending the garden, which was up and thriving. For Allan it was fencing, milking, or cutting firewood.

One morning Jean set about to thin the carrots.

Ross watched her for a few moments and then asked, "Mummy, why are you pulling out all the baby carrots?"

"Well Ross, carrots are just like little boys, they need lots of room to grow."

Allan had an outdoor stove in the yard, three feet long and two feet high, that he used, on occasion, for scalding chickens. He would get a fire roaring in the stove and heat a deep copper canner full of water. He would kill the chickens by chopping their heads off with the axe. This was horrifying to any of the children who happened to be about, especially if the chickens would run around after their heads were cut off. Allan was careful to kill the chickens when the boys were not about, however, as he realized how easily terrified the kids were. The chickens were then dipped into scalding water, which loosened the feathers, and then they were easily plucked.

Allan had bought a horse from Charlie Haight, a nearby neighbor, and Jean, thinking her, at first, to be a lovely looking animal, had named her Jess in honor of Allan's late mother. Jess though was balky and as stubborn as if she had been born a mule. Shortly after they got her Allan told Jean, "That horse is dumber than a sack of hammers!" One morning she refused to back into the buggy traces, and no amount of coaxing could encourage her to budge. Finally, in frustration, Allan grabbed her bridle and twisted it tight around her muzzle, and then by sheer force and a well-placed shove along her flank, he pushed her back into the traces.

"Stand still you darn fool or you'll end up in the frozen food locker!"

Quivering she obeyed.

Lanny holding the reins, Leslie Little and Alan Varga with Jess pulling the wagon.

In the summer, Allan would water her, then ride her over to a field around the corner and tether her to an old tire he had carted there. She would eat around the tire in a circle and then drag it over and eat another circle. He would bring her home on his way back from the milk route, and depending on the weather, stable her in the barn or leave her in the corral. One summer Saturday, Jean's sister, Margaret, her husband Tony, and their children Carole, Bud, and Rick came to visit.

They were all out in the yard under the shade trees when they heard a terrified whiney, followed by the thudding of hoofs on gravel. A bear had wandered into the field, and Jess, on smelling him, had reacted in terror. She fled the field, charging down the road towards the house dragging the tire behind her. Every few feet, the tire would crash into her, eliciting new terror and a sputtering stream of flatulence. What a spectacle! All the family watched in shock except little Cousin Rick, who fell to the ground overcome with laughter.

Reacting quickly, Allan ran to the truck and, calling for Tony, they raced down the road after her. When she began to run out of steam, they were able to pull in front of her. Allan got her loose from the tire and led her back home.

A less frequent visitor to the farm than Margaret, Tony and family, was Allan's cousin Herbert Grant. He was a bachelor born in 1884, who had fought in both WW1 and with the International Brigade in the Spanish Civil War. Now, he lived off his pension and prospected. He was tall, bone thin, and wore, with his battered suit, a dress shirt buttoned to the neck but no tie. He smelled faintly of pine soap and strongly of pipe tobacco. Whenever he really got hungry, he would come by and spend a few days with Jean and Allan. His favorite meal was chicken and dumplings, and Jean always made sure to fix it for him. On one visit, Jean had made lemon meringue pies and, bringing just one to the table dished everyone but Herbert a slice.

"Oh Herbert this is terrible, we are all out!"

Poor Herbert looked completely stricken! Laughing, Jean rushed to get the other pie, and, feeling bad about her trick, she gave Herbert a second piece. Allan chuckled all through dessert, surprised that Jean would pull a trick on company.

Herbert and a neighbor of Jean and Allan's, old Mr. Wheatherall, had decidedly different political leanings. As Mr. Wheatherall walked into town every weekday, Herbert would lie in wait for his return hike up the road and 'just happen' to be in the vicinity. He would strike up a conversation, which would soon turn into an argument. Jean was mortified and did everything in her power to prevent these altercations by baking some delicious morsel in a vain attempt to distract Herbert. Robin and Ross looked forward to the old man's visits. They were assured a tasty treat and a rousing argument.

Chapter 7

The hot summer days ripened the wild berries. Jean would give Robin and Ross each a metal bucket to carry and they would set off into the woods, with her carrying Lanny in search of a blackberry patch, a huckleberry or Oregon grape bush, or an Elderberry tree. Sparky trailed along behind as fast as his little legs would allow.

The boys would eat most of the berries they picked, so to keep Lanny busy Jean would have them pick for him. She smiled to see them sprawled on the moss like little wood sprites, their mouths all stained purple. She would pick as fast as she could to fill the buckets. The boys would carry them home for her, and the afternoon was spent boiling the berries down over a hot fire to make pints of dark purple blackberry jam or Oregon grape jelly or bright red elderberry jelly or huckleberry jam.

The neighboring Bodner family had a huge strawberry field and, when the season was about over they would let the neighbors come in to glean the fields. She was able to get six lovely pints of strawberry jam to add to her stores.

Jean had a small washtub she would half fill with water for the boys to paddle their feet in on hot summer days when she was busy in the kitchen. One afternoon she heard Vera Masuravitch laughing and calling out, "Sons of freedom, sons of freedom," a reference to a splinter group from the Doukhobors (a group of Russian refugees who had settled in the interior of B.C. in 1899 and whose practices included nudity as a form of political protest). She popped her head out the door to see that baby Lanny had stripped all his clothes off to enjoy the water better.

Lanny in all his glory.

The neighbors visited back and forth a lot, especially the women. They would help each other with big projects like quilting or canning, or just drop by for a cup of tea.

Besides company, the most welcome diversion was a letter. This day's mail brought an informative one from Grace. She could not wait until Allan got home that afternoon to read it to him! There was news indeed! The rest of the afternoon seemed to drag by unmercifully. Finally, he got in from the milk run. He chased the boys a few times around the yard, teasing them with the threat of a whisker rub. They shrieked in mock terror. Lanny, although only ten months was already toddling and he loved to join in the play with his brothers.

She took the letter outside and called to him, "Allan, we have a letter from Grace!"

"Well, what does she have to say for herself?"

"You'll never guess! She's getting married!"

He paused in his play and took a drink of water from the aluminum dipper that hung on the side of the porch water bucket. "What, to whom?"

"Oh Allan, to Walter of course!"

He chuckled, "Well, good for her!"

Jean continued, "You'll never guess what day she's chosen!"

"No," he drawled, "I probably never will. You're just going to have to tell me."

"October the 12th." Just in case, he had forgotten the significance of that occasion she added, "Your birthday!"

"Will there be cake?" Robin hollered.

"Cake!" Chorused Ross.

Jean was especially delighted for Grace and started right away to embroider some pillowcases and crochet around the edges of them as a wedding gift.

The summer days brought a few trips to Hayward or Hatzic Lake to swim. One day at Hayward Lake, where they had gone for a picnic, Robin and Ross were wading while Jean changed Lanny into his swim trunks. Ross walked into a deep hole and plunged in over his head.

Robin immediately started yelling "Ross, you better come out of there!"

Jean turned and plunged into the water, pulling Ross to safety and ruining a perfectly good set of shoes and a watch in the process.

Sometimes they let the older boys stay up late to see the stars. They would pull two chairs outside in the yard. Without a light for miles, the stars were amazingly bright. Robin would sit on Allan's lap and Ross on Jean's while they pointed out the constellations. The stillness of the evenings was breathtaking.

Ross picnicking in the yard.

Late summer dinners were full of vegetables from their garden, which they loved to eat smothered in butter. Fall came all too soon, and there was a flurry of canning for Jean. The boys had to play in the yard and watch Lanny while Jean canned. Grace came one weekend, and they got all the pickled beets, beans, peas, applesauce, and pears done. It was such a relief to Jean to have the canning all finished. She would gaze at the rows of jars each time she opened her well-stocked cupboards. They had a good crop of carrots, cabbages and potatoes, which they stored in their dirt basement.

Allan had a tall, long double stacked row of wood cut for the stove. He had cut hay for the cattle down at the Little's field with a hand scythe. It would not last the whole winter. He would have to buy some when it ran out, but it filled their small hayloft.

They were surprised to find a hazelnut tree up on the hill. They had planted a walnut tree, but it had not produced anything this year. However, the mature hazelnut provided them with nuts that the boys loved to try to crack on the floor with Allan's hammer.

October came at last, and the family traveled to Crescent Beach for Walter and Grace's wedding. Grace had made her dress, but more importantly to the boys, had also made a beautiful two layer, dark fruitcake wedding cake as was traditional in Canada. They were married in the yard of Walter's home.

Jean could not have been happier for her dear friend and sister-in-law. Allan hugged his sister and wished her well. At the bride's request, he had brought his fiddle and played a number of dance songs for the gathering. Jean was immensely proud of him. They stayed to help clean up the dishes, so it was late when the little family returned to the farm.

Allan carried the two older boys in, one by one, Ross asleep and Robin just pretending, while Jean carried Lanny. While she got them changed and tucked into bed, Allan hurried off to milk the lowing cows by moonlight. That was the only trouble with a farm; it made it almost impossible to go anywhere.

They celebrated Lanny's birthday the following week quietly with just the family and the present of a cast iron toy dump truck. Lanny called it a 'ruck.' He pushed it around the floor beneath the table and chairs most of that day. Thanksgiving was just around the corner and they planned on a big dinner over at Jack's with all the family.

Fall settled in and with it came rain. Jean kept the boys busy helping her around the house. She taught them to help knead bread and to churn butter. Her enormous blue enamel bread pan was big enough to hold all three of the boys. Why they had not already dragged it outside for a boat was a wonder, but when it was not in use, Jean had it safely hung on a nail high enough on the wall to be out of their reach.

When done with the chores, they would all climb up on Mummy and Daddy's big double bed to read stories. If she was lucky, one or two of them might fall asleep. When it was not raining, she would bundle them up and take them for long walks in the woods. Lanny could walk very well holding her hand, and they would walk until he was tired. Then she would carry him home. She would point out the geese flying overhead and the huge fungi growing on the tree trunks. On those fall walks they would search for the perfect Christmas tree and memorize how to find it again when Christmas came.

To the delight of the boys, Christmas finally did come. Both Grandma and Auntie Grace sent Christmas presents, mostly clothing for the coming year. Grace always knit Robin a sweater every year, and he passed his old one down to Ross and so on to Lanny. They were grateful for the gift of a ham Uncle Jack brought from the pigs on his farm.

Allan bought Jean a rocking chair, and Jean knit Allan several pair of wool socks. They got the boys a few toys and filled their stockings, which they hung, with oranges and candies. The tree, with candles in golden colored holders, was only lighted for a few hours, after dark, on Christmas Eve and Christmas day. Jean taught the children the Christmas story with a small nativity set which she would then let them handle by themselves. It became a Christmas treasure.

"Well Jean, our first year on the farm is almost over," Allan mused as they cuddled into bed at the end of the day.

"Yes, it's been a good year, hasn't it?"

He drew her close and kissed her. "Yes, it certainly has."

Chapter 8

Allan was determined to build a bigger hayloft for next winter. He set to work on cutting down eight of the tallest and straightest trees he could find. They would form the four corners and four support columns of his hayloft, which he was building directly behind the existing barn. He overlaid the columns with rafters and finally covered them with plywood to form a typical barn or Gambrel roof. It was an ambitious project and took most of the winter, spring, and early summer to complete. However, it finally was finished in 1949, and the huge cavernous roof, without walls, would hold plenty of hay for all his livestock.

However, one night he expressed concern to Jean that the uprights were possibly not adequately braced to hold the weight of the roof.

"What are you going to do about it, Allan?"

"I think I can brace them with some cables. I'll pick some up next time I'm in town."

On his next day off from the milk run (he was spelled two day a week by a 'relief' driver), he drove into town to pick up some heavy wire cables. He went to work attaching two bands of them with staples to the corner uprights and then proceeded twisting them together, like a turnbuckle, between the two support columns with a stout green stick. It was like two giant elastic bands around the four poles across the front of the barn. It was working well until one leg of his large step- ladder dropped into a mouse hole.

Allan lost his hold on the stick, causing the cables to unwind and catch his thumb, nearly tearing it loose from his hand. He managed to get hold of the winding stick again before the cable tore his thumb completely off and call for Jean. Luckily, she heard him hollering and, running to the barn, found him hanging on for dear life, both arms over the cable, sixteen feet up in the air. Unable to lift the tall ladder, she ran to Gabe and Vera's calling for help. Down the road she ran, clambered over the fence, all the while calling "Gabe! Gabe!"

Gabe heard her yelling and came out the door of his barn. She motioned frantically for him to come, shouting. "It's Allan!"

She wheeled around and ran for home. All the way home she was praying, "Please God, don't let him fall!" She could hear Gabe puffing behind her, his heavy work boots thudding the ground. He caught up to her just as they were entering the yard.

"Vere is he?"

"The barn," she gasped, pointing.

She could hardly breathe by the time she made it back. Robin was standing in the barn staring up at his Daddy and calling out encouragingly, "Hold on Daddy!" Blood from Allan's torn thumb was dripping down to the dirt floor of the barn. The pain was pulsing through his hand with every heartbeat, but Allan was more aware of the cutting pressure of the cable under his armpits than the throbbing hand. Between Gabe and Jean, they were able to lift the ladder, get Allan's hand free from the cable, and load him in the truck.

Gabe did not drive; his only mode of transport was a bicycle, so Jean hollered to Robin, "Watch your brothers!" She jumped in

61

the driver's seat and, gears grinding headed down the road to Little's. Wally Little was at home and volunteered to drive Allan, in his own car, to the hospital.

Robin stood there a minute, staring after the departing truck, and then looked at Gabe, who was already headed to his fence line. He scratched at his elbow then turned and looked at the house. Mummy had made Ross stay inside today because he had been coughing in the night. He sighed and then headed inside. He looked in their bedroom and saw Lanny was sleeping in the crib. Ross was sitting in the big armchair looking at a picture book. Robin sat in a kitchen chair and stared at him. Ross looked up. "Whatcha doing?"

"Watching you."

Ross looked down again at the book then, looking up, asked "Why?"

"Mummy said."

Ross stared at him. "Where is Mummy?"

Robin sighed, "She left in the truck."

Ross continued to stare. "Is it lunch time yet?"

"I dunno."

"Can you make me a peanut blah blah sandwich?"

Robin turned and looked forlornly at the counter. He could see the red and yellow metal breadbox, and he knew he could reach it, but cutting the bread was another thing altogether. Mummy had told him he had better not *ever* touch the big bread knife. He frowned. "No, I don't think so."

After seeing Allan safely on his way, Jean hurried back to the farm. Robin heard the truck door slam and jumped up to look out the window. "Mummy's home!"

Robin, Ross, Lanny.

Fortunately, a Dr. Marcellus was able to save Allan's thumb. About two hours later Wally brought him home. Jean put him to bed, under protest, for the remainder of the day.

That afternoon Margaret and Tony's family came out from Vancouver. With the disaster of the morning, Jean had forgotten all about their impending visit. Robin spied them arriving and ran out to meet them at the gate calling out cheerfully, "Hey, Auntie Marg, Daddy hung himself in the barn!"

A shocked Marg and Tony rushed to the house while Robin took his unconcerned cousins off to see his newest fort.

"Jean, what happened?" Marg demanded as they entered the house.

Jean was surprised to see them but greeted them with a smile and explained the goings on of the morning.

"Robin said his Daddy hung himself!" Margaret burst out.

"Oh, that little imp! Well, I suppose in a way, he's right."

It was several weeks until Allan had full use of that hand, so Wally's wife, Helen Little, came up twice a day to help Jean with the milking. From that day on, the Little's were provided with all the milk they could use.

While Allan was laid up, the boys convinced him to tell them stories about when he was a little boy.

"When I was 10 years old," Allan began," we lived in the small prairie town of Foxwarren, Manitoba. One day I had a terrible toothache, and since there was no dentist in our town, Doc Lanigan was called to the house to do the job. They sat me on a kitchen chair, and there was a hot fire in the old tin heater, so it must have been in the middle of the winter. Doc Lanigan proceeded to try to pull that tooth and nearly pulled my head off instead. Finally, the tooth gave way; the Doc fell backwards and sat his behind on the hot stove. I can still remember the smell of his clothing scorching on that heater, and he lost no time getting away from it. I thought it was very funny and had a good laugh. It helped me forget the sore tooth as there was no anesthetic to be had in those days."

Allan hauling firewood about 1914.

"Another story Daddy!" Ross and Robin chorused together.

"Just one more, and then its bedtime. When I was about 8 years old, a robin built her nest at the top of a telegraph pole near our farm. I was determined to see if there were eggs in it, so one day I shinnied up the pole, and sure enough, there were three bright blue eggs in the nest. I wanted to take one home with me, so I picked one up, but having no place to carry it, I had to pop it into my mouth. I shinnied back down the pole, and when I dropped onto the ground, that egg in my mouth broke! Yuck!"

"Ewe yucky," cried the boys.

Allan was off two weeks from the milk run. He applied for and received unemployment insurance. He took Robin and Ross with him to the Unemployment office to pick up his check. There was a long lineup for checks, so Allan left the boys in the truck and went and stood in line outside the building. It took considerable time for Allan to work his way through the line to where he disappeared from view into the interior of the building.

"I can't see Dad," Ross said looking across the street at the lineup of strange men.

"It's O.K. He is in the building to get his check." Robin answered.

"I don't know. It's been a long time."

"It isn't that long," Robin said disagreeably.

"I am going to yell for Dad!"

"No, don't!" Robin was getting agitated now himself. He was supposed to be in charge and keep things under control.

Ross made his mind up. "Yeah, I am going to yell for Dad!"

"No, don't yell!"

"Dad!" Ross hollered at the top of his lungs.

"Please, Ross, shut up!" Robin yelled at the top of *his* lungs.

"DAAAAAAAD!" Ross yelled again and Robin realized the first attempt had not been any-where near at the top of his lungs.

People walking by the truck stopped to stare, and, across the street, the men in line looked over. Robin realized he was going to be in trouble.

Ross's next yell almost lifted the roof off the truck, "DAAAAAAAAAD!" The veins in his neck stood out. His face turned bright red, and tears trailed down to his chin.

At the same time, Robin began yelling out the window at the people who were staring. "Go away, and leave him alone! He is all right. Do not get him excited!"

Eventually, Allan, having the person behind him save his place in line, came out to the truck and calmed the boys down. Finally, Allan got his check and returned to Nelson Road. The boys did not go into town near so often anymore with their Dad.

Allan was soon back driving the milk truck and throwing the heavy cans on and off without using his thumb. Jean was upset about him going back so soon, but she was powerless to stop him. On his last visit to Dr. Marcellus, to get the stitches out, the doctor asked him if he could touch his palm with the tip of his thumb. Allan tried but could only touch the upper part of his palm by the base of his little finger.

"Oh, that's too bad," Doc commiserated.

"Why?" replied Allan and then showed Doc he could only do the same with his other hand!

That summer was dry, and Allan was hauling water for the cattle from the stream before it was halfway thru July. The pasture was getting bare as well; he did not know how much longer he could keep the five cows fed. He had noticed a lush field down at the bottom of Nelson Hill, bordering Silver Creek. He finally stopped one day on the way past Ernie Nelson's to ask him about it. It belonged to Ernie, and he told Allan he had no problem with him summering his cattle there. Allan went right home and saddled up Jess, tied the cattle in a string and led them down to the pasture. An added benefit was that he could store and sell the unused part of the evening milking by setting the milk cans in the stream to keep them cool. He no longer had to worry about feeding and watering the stock but now would have to get up an hour earlier to make it down to do the milking and get to the milk route on time.

The boys all celebrated their birthday that summer on the same day. Jean had found chaps, vests, and cowboy hats for the three of them, and all summer long they were cowboys. Allan picked up a gentle little brown pony at a horse farm for the boys to ride, and they named her Star for the white marking on her forehead.

Robin, Lanny and Ross

The boys came up with a great game called the Pony Express. The rider would come charging in to the Station (the front porch), jump onto a fresh horse, and ride away as if all the Indians and Outlaws of the west were after him. The only problem was there were no fresh horses, only a fresh rider. Star became increasingly bored with the game.

Robin hopped on her back, for the fifth time, and gave her a good kick in the ribs with his imaginary spurs. Star took off like a shot. She almost cleared the page wire fence that ran around the house yard, all except one front hoof. She did a complete somersault with Robin hanging on for dear life and landed on her back with Robin pinned halfway beneath her. The saddle horn completely knocked the wind out of him. He lay there gasping for breath. Star was also quite winded. She had attempted a rather monumental feat for a small pony, but she managed to roll off Robin and stagger to her feet. Ross began hollering for Jean. He was sure Robin had killed himself this time. Fortunately, both boy and pony survived to ride another day.

That year Robin turned five. Ross turned three, and Lanny turned two. By late November, Jean was expecting their fourth child.

Ross, Lanny and Robin.

Chapter 9

In early spring of 1950, Jean drove into town to consult with Dr Marcellus. He told her what she already knew, and they set the due date for late in July.

They were definitely going to outgrow the Dodge truck, so Allan started looking around for a car. He found a 1931 Model A 4-door sedan, took Jean to look at it, and then brought it home. The boys were ecstatic with the novelty of a back seat; all three could ride comfortably with lots of room between.

Jeans mother would come watch the boys while their mother went in the hospital for a week and even stay an additional week. Grace wrote to say that she and Walter would come get the two older boys when Grandma went home and have them for a week in White Rock. July came and went with no baby, but August 1 brought a new little brother for the boys. They were thrilled, and their cousin, Stan, was envious! Grandma was a terrific baby sitter. She took the boys on hikes, to the lake and down into the gully to play—all the things that Jean had not felt up to doing for the past several months.

They named the new baby John Bruce, John being a family name on both sides and Bruce being a Scottish whim of Jean's. He was a healthy, happy baby, and Jean tried to adjust to having four little boys around the house. Grace and Walter arrived bearing gifts two weeks after the birth. They stayed just a few hours then loaded up Robin (now six) and Ross (four) and took them back to Crescent Beach.

Ross, Lanny and Grandma Jane Peebles.

The boys had all kinds of new adventures including going to a beach covered in white rocks. They picked up seashells and sand dollars. They listened to the gleaming white gulls shrieking and watched them drop shells onto the rocks to crack them open. It was their first time to smell the salty air of the ocean. They ran and played in the waves with delighted abandon. There was a huge 120-ton boulder painted white gracing the beach. Of course, Robin had to try climbing it. Grace bought them fish and chips that they dipped in little white paper cups filled with tangy brown vinegar.

Auntie Grace had a shed with a low roof in her back yard, and Robin was positive he could ride the blue tricycle, provided that week for their enjoyment, off the roof of the shed and not come

71

to any bodily harm. Ross was not quite so sure, but if Robin was willing to try, he was willing to help haul the trike up there. They found a few boards and buckets to assist in their endeavor and would have succeeded in gaining the rooftop had a yelling Auntie Grace not intercepted them. As for Grace, she was beginning to understand why Allan yelled at the boys on a regular basis.

Towards the end of the week, Auntie Grace announced that the next day they would ride the bus into town and attend the movie theater. It would be the first time they had done either. The boys whooped and hollered. The half hour bus ride was a novelty for the two little boys who sat glued to the window, firing off questions about what they saw to their Aunt.

Auntie Grace had chosen the only movie available that week in their little town of White Rock, "The Man from Planet X." The boys both were fine until the scene where a woman looks in the window of a flying saucer, downed on the Scottish moors, and sees an alien face with a background of eerie sounding music. She immediately began screaming, and Ross scooted out of his seat and hid under it for the duration, offering up an occasional, "Don't look, Robin!" and "I don't like the sound of this," whenever the music would crescendo. Robin put both hands over his face and watched the movie occasionally through his fingers when he did not have his eyes completely shut. Now and again Robin would jump down out of his seat to say encouraging things to Ross, but Ross did not move until the house lights came back up. Grace sat and chuckled to herself through the whole movie.

The bus ride home was a lot less fun than the ride to the movie had been. The boys were sure something evil was lurking in the dark. Instead of their noses against the window, they had their little bodies pressed as close as they could get one on either side of their ample Auntie Grace. Then there was the terrifying walk two blocks home from the bus to the house. If Grace were making sure the boys would be happy to return home to the farm, she had done a good job.

The end of the summer brought the end of Robin's carefree childhood and the beginning of school. The bus stop was a half mile away, and Robin walked with the rest of the neighborhood kids, the Bodners, the Vargas, and the Sporries. They called themselves the Nelson Road Gang. They were too far from either Mission City or Silverdale to feel like they belonged to either place. Robin started grade one in the basement of the Anglican Church on 2nd Avenue in Mission, that was built in 1901.

One day Robin was having an intense argument with Nina Masuravich on the way to the bus, and she finally yelled in exasperation, "Robin Irwin the whole world does not revolve around you!"

He looked around at the woods, the hay fields, and the strawberry fields, the horizon an equal distance in every direction, and thought to himself, "It most certainly does!"

One day that autumn as Allan came up Nelson Hill on the milk route, he could see that Ernie's milk cans were not out at his stand yet.

"Ernie's up late today," he muttered to himself.

He drove by and went on up the road to pick up Gabe's and his own milk cans, and then came back down to Ernie's stop. He could see, even from a distance, the milk cans were still not at the stand. Pulling the truck as close to the barn as he could, he stopped and jumped down from the cab. He could hear cows lowing in the barn, and he recognized the sound. They wanted milking! He glanced down the long center corridor of the huge red barn and called out, "Ernie!" There was no answering shout.

Allan turned and ran towards the farmhouse, stopping only to wipe his feet. He opened the back door and called, "Ernie!" Again, no reply. He raced through the messy kitchen, cluttered living room, and headed up the stairs all the while calling out for him. There were several doorways off the landing at the top of the stairs. He headed to the one that was slightly ajar. He found the old fellow in bed with pneumonia too weak to call out. Allan saw to his immediate needs and reassured him that he would take care of the cows and, as soon as he reached a phone, would call an ambulance. He worked like a mad man for the next hour and a half to milk Ernie's herd, turn them out to pasture, and load the milk cans.

He sped down the hill to the next stop. Because he was so late, the farmer was hovering near the stand watching for him. He helped Allan load the heavy milk cans and Allan explained Ernie's dire situation. "I've got a neighbor with a phone. I'll run down there right now and have the ambulance come get him," the man offered.

For the two weeks it took Ernie to get back on his feet, Allan took over his chores and milking, as well as his own. Ernie recovered and ran his dairy for another 3 years until 1953. His land was later purchased to build the Mission Golf Course and Ernie had his homestead farmhouse moved, near the bottom of the hill, closer to Silver Creek.

Daisy, one of Allan's cows, had been inseminated the previous fall, and she had a lovely calf that spring. He was a headstrong little fellow, and one day when Robin had him on a lead rope, the calf spied the corral gate open. He took off running through the gate, across the yard, and out onto Nelson Road with Robin hanging on for all he was worth. Robin could hear his Dad hollering something about the rope, so he hung on to it!

Unable to keep up, he fell to the ground and slid on his belly in the gravel almost to the Masuravich's driveway. By then his elbows and knees were skinned, and he determined that a licking from Dad could not be worse than this. Besides, if he ruined the school shoes he was wearing, Mum would skin him alive. He let go of the rope, and that darn rascal of a calf stopped running and nonchalantly began to eat the lush grass at the side of the road. Allan caught up to Robin, and, helping him to stand and, examining his scrapes, said in exasperation, "Why didn't you let go of the rope?" Robin just stared at him open mouthed and wondered if he was ever going to learn the right thing to do.

Something had startled Allan awake. He lay still and listened intently. There it was. A moan and a sob. He turned over slowly to not waken Jean and swung his legs out of bed. The floor was cold. He walked softly to the boys' bedroom door in his nighttime attire of white, button front, long johns. He could see the boys were covered up. He determined it was Robin moaning and, thinking he was having nightmares told him, "Its O.K. Go back to sleep." He went and added more wood to the fire before heading back to bed.

A feverish Robin told his Mummy the next day, "A giant polar bear came and talked to me last night."

"Really? What did he say?"

"He told me to go back to sleep."

Many a night thereafter, Jean sat up with both Robin and Ross and finally in desperation took them to see Dr. Marcellus. The Doctor's office was up a long flight of stairs in a building right on Main Street. He was a cheerful, handsome man dressed formally in a shirt, tie, and spotless white lab coat. He diagnosed the boys with tonsillitis, prescribed Penicillin, and then, removal of the tonsils as soon as the boys were well enough.

Therefore, in several weeks the two boys were off to Mission Memorial Hospital for a week's stay. They had to provide their own pajamas and were each allowed to take a favorite toy. Robin's bed was in a long hallway next to a water fountain, and Ross's was in a nearby ward. Just as Robin walked in the door to Ross's ward, a little bully there took Ross's toy donkey and cart away and threw it across the room. Robin took on the role of protector; put the fear of death in the boy, and the young fellow did not bother Ross again.

Dr. Marcellus removed their tonsils early the next day, and the boys were up and around by the afternoon. Ross scooted down out of bed and went in search of Robin. Finding him in the hall, he complained to his brother, "I don't like the ladies here. They keep sticking me."

Robin scrunched over in bed and, lifting the blankets said, "Climb in here, Ross. You can hide under the covers."

The nurses were soon in an uproar searching for their little lost patient. When Ross was finally discovered, the boys were no longer viewed with much sympathy.

The next day Robin, being so close to the water fountain, decided it would be a good idea to have a drinking contest. The boys decided whoever could drink the most water would be the champion. They would each guzzle as much as they could until they had to come up for air, and then it would be the other's turn. They both, however, started heaving about the same time, so the winner was undecided. Besides, neither one of them felt like celebrating a victory.

Christmas 1951 John Bruce.

Chapter 10

1951

One of the interesting neighbors at the farm was Miss Beatrice Stewart. She was very reclusive. Though she was geographically one of their closest neighbors, the families did not interact. She was in possession of the ugliest, scariest dog the world had ever seen. He was black and white, with short, mangy hair and long legs. He was also blind in one eye. Robin and Ross did not walk past Miss Stewart's house. They ran. She did have, however, an enticing field with a large unused barn surrounded by woods that the boys found hard to resist. Every so often, when they happened to tire exploring their own 18-acre wood, they would sneak across the road into hers. This forbidden activity was exhilaratingly scary for a five and six year old.

One day they were brave enough, or should we say stupid enough, to go beyond the woods and attempt to cross the field to her barn. The dog caught wind of them as they were about center field and ran to intercept them. The boys flattened themselves in the tall grass and hoped for the best. The dog ran in an ever-decreasing circle around the field, searching for them, but he had his blind eye towards them, so he never did catch a glimpse. (This is probably where the old adage "turning a blind eye" came from.) The boys determined that they would have to make a run for it, and when the dog was at the far end of the field, they made a mad dash for the road and home. They never looked back until they were in the safety of their own yard. For all they knew, the dog was still running in circles.

This was the summer that Jean started letting the older boys sleep out side. It became a treasured summer tradition. They loved to be out in the dark and watch the stars. Sometimes they were lucky enough to see a falling star. Jean trusted Sparky to be their watchdog; he was excessively protective of the boys. If Allan spanked one of the boys' outside, Sparky would growl and bite at his arm.

Unbeknown to Jean and Allan, the boys started another tradition at this time known, in later years, as the "sock wars." They would wait until their parents were asleep for the night then fill their long socks with pinecones. They would chase each other around the yard, swinging the socks high above their heads to try to knock each other senseless.

They produced most of their food themselves on the farm. Allan built hutches and bought some big white rabbits' at auction. The boys loved the gentle soft bunnies, and they were a lovely variation from chicken. The first night Jean served it for dinner, Robin asked, "Is this chicken?"

Allan took another bite and raised his eyebrows to Jean. Clearly, he was going to let her fend for herself on this one. Jean looked down at her plate then looked up and calmly said, "Yes, Robin, it's chicken."

"Oh, O.K."

She looked across the table at Allan. Allan smiled at her and shot her a wink.

There were a few staples like flour and sugar that they bought a month's worth at a time. These Jean stored in huge white metal cans. Ross was with his Mum one day at the grocery store when the total came to $22 dollars. Jean gave an audible gasp. Ross was afraid she was going to start to cry, right there in the store, but she held it in. Their grocery budget for the month was $20.

Allan had subscribed to a newspaper, *The Vancouver Sun*, and Jean read the grocery adds diligently. When she saw an add featuring a product they needed but was limited to one per customer, she would load up all the kids and take them to the Overwaitie, give them each the money to pay for the limited item and send them through the line while she brought up the rear. The manager never complained about the little customers.

The boys were strictly forbidden to be anywhere nearby when Allan was cutting down trees. Little Lanny would stand watching out the window on such occasions and say, "There goes Daddy, making more stumps." Allan's days off were often spent clearing the acreage. He would back the truck into the pit he had dug into the side of the small hill. With a gas-operated circular saw at the top of the pit and a chute to slide the wood down into the truck, he soon had a load of wood to take into town to sell door to door.

He had a wood delivery run up to the Stave Lake area. It was always miserably cold up that valley, at least at the time of year when people wanted firewood. He had unloaded the wood and was headed back home, whistling. Bam! The truck skidded right and then left before Allan could wrestle it to a stop. Reaching for his leather work gloves, he jumped from the cab, reached over the seat and pulled out the jack.

"Darn it all to heck!"

What a place to get a flat tire. He was in the middle of nowhere.

He glanced at the rear tire. He was going to have to hurry up about it; he had only about another hour of daylight. He hustled around to the other side of the cab and pulled his tire irons and patch kit out of the glove box. He jacked up the truck and removed the tire, carefully placing the lug nuts on the truck bed. Using his homemade tire irons, he began prying the tire off the outside edge of the rim. He was irritated to see the hole in the inner tube was much larger than his patches would handle.

He looked around at his surroundings, wondering what he could use to fill the tire. There, about twenty feet down the road, was a pile of sand. Small sand piles were routinely left alongside the road at intervals for drivers to use under their tires if they were stuck in the snow. Slinging the damaged inner tube over his shoulder, he rolled the tire down to the sand pile. He proceeded to pack the inner tube tightly with sand. The blow out hole presented somewhat of a problem until he thought of wrapping it tightly with his pocket-handkerchief. It would wear it threadbare, but if it got him home, it would be worth the sacrifice.

He was dog-tired by the time he got the tire back on the rim. He felt the first drops of a drizzle of rain beginning. Rolling the tire back awkwardly to the truck, he held out hope that this idea was actually going to work. He quickly replaced the tire and tightened the lug nuts in the growing dusk.

Hopping back in the truck, he placed all his tools next to him on the seat. He might have need of them again soon. Starting up the truck, he rolled it slowly down to the sand pile. Grabbing his short handled shovel out of its spot on the truck bed, he shoveled enough sand into the truck to refill the tire if he needed to. Checking the rear wheel one last time, he drove slowly home, taking extra caution to avoid the potholes.

He was amazed when he rolled into the yard that it had actually gotten him all the way home. Jean was worried and had kept his dinner warm for him. He would have to show her the tire in the morning; he doubted she would believe him when he told her.

When Allan would run out of money and a tire would need replacing he would take another old tire, cut off the sidewalls, fit it inside the first tire, reinsert the inner tube, pump it up and off he would go. He was also adept at making engine bearings out of leather when he did not have the money to replace them. On occasions such as these, he would say to Jean, "I've got a new patent!"

He had his own quiet way of dealing with those who would try to take advantage of him on a sale of wood. One afternoon he had just finished unloading a cord of wood when the buyer told him it didn't seem like enough and offered to pay only a part of the agreed upon price.

Allan said, "Well you can stack it and measure it, and if it is less than a cord, I will bring you more."

The man refused to do so and insisted Allan accept less money for it. Allan simply began to reload the wood in his truck. When the man realized he intended to take it all back, he paid him the agreed upon price and walked away. Allan would never deliver wood there again. Irish blood runs thick.

Allan loved to eat, especially Jeans chocolate cakes. He would cut the butter cream icing off and save it for last. The boys began imitating this. Allan would point in mock horror to the far kitchen wall and exclaim, "What is that!" The boys would turn to look at this imaginary diversion, and Allan would steal the icing off their plates. In self-defense, they began eating their frosting first.

If Allan heard Robin telling the boys ghost stories in bed at night, he would take a bed sheet, sneak outside, hang the sheet over a long stick, and wave it by the boys' bedroom window. It was usually effective at getting Robin to stop.

Robin delighted in scaring his younger brothers, and one of his ingenious inventions was "the witch tree". This was a huge old maple to the east of the barn, near the chicken coop, that had a large dead branch halfway up. Lanny was not sure if the branch, which remotely resembled a witches' nose, was the witches' perch or her nose, or if the whole tree was the witch. Lanny believed his brother. It was a very scary tree, especially at twilight.

Another of Robin's creative stories was "The Cabbage that Ate Chicago". It had scared Lanny, who was just turning four that October, out of his wits. This was unknown to Jean, and one fall day, the garden already harvested, she sent Lanny to go to the root cellar basement to get potatoes for dinner. Lanny knew there were cabbages stored there as well. He stood out in the yard staring at the basement door. There was just no way he was going down in that dank, dark, dirt-floored dungeon filled with people eating cabbages. Jean peeked out the kitchen door to see what was keeping him. He looked up at her with fear—filled eyes. The look melted her heart. She took him by the hand and went with him to the dark cellar to fetch the potatoes. She saw him cast a terrified eye at the wooden box full of cabbages.

"That's funny," she thought to herself, "I wonder why a child would be frightened of those."

Allan came home one day with a huge roll of dark green linoleum that he had seen at a rock bottom price. With Jack's help, they moved all the furniture outside, including the mammoth stove, and covered all the floors in the kitchen, living area, and hall with the wonderful smooth flooring.

Jean was ecstatic! It was so easy to clean compared to the wood plank floors. The boys loved to run down the hall and slide across the dining area and thump up against the front door. Jean began to think this was their best "toy" ever. One day she noticed a dark spot on the floor and, reaching down to remove it, discovered it was a small hole about the size of a penny. It went all the way through to the wood planking. Horrified, she called all the boys together and demanded, "Who put this hole in the floor?"

Robin looked up at her with wide blue innocent eyes, "I did Mummy."

"Why ever would you do that Robin?"

"It's the pit to back my truck into, so I can load my cows and horses." He could have just have easily have added, "of course."

Jean took a deep breath and calmly but rather loudly explained, "You can go outside and dig all the holes you want, but no one is to dig any more holes in the floor! Understand?"

The boys had another adventure that summer involving Miss Beatrice Stewart's property. Not seeing her mangy dog anywhere visible for several days, they made a sneak attack and, crawling on their bellies made it all the way to her barn. Their objective was simply exploratory. However, Ross happened to spy a chain on the ground that ran beneath the closed barn door, and, thinking it was something he could put to good use, he reached down, grabbed it, and began to pull. The boys soon came to understand that, attached to the other end, was the "devil dog".

Chapter 11

1952

The family started out the New Year with a party at Uncle Jack's that went late into the evening. Grandma and Granddad Peebles came out from Vancouver, and they had some exciting news. They were selling their home and moving to the eighty acres in Tulameen B.C. that they had purchased just after the war. Two of their sons, Morris and Bob, owned a sawmill on the property and were building them a log home from the ponderosa pine that covered their land. Situated on a hill overlooking the Tulameen River, the property was in a beautiful spot, some 160 miles north of Mission. Grandma had always dreamed of having a log home. Granddad would be leaving in the spring to go up and help the boys finish the house, which was to have a flush toilet and hot and cold running water!

It was a merry party. Allan, of course, had brought his fiddle, and they danced in the New Year. Jean could not help being secretly envious of her mother—what she would not give to have running water and an indoor toilet. However, there was no way they could afford those luxuries just yet. She was grateful Allan had a job, and they always were able to make do with what they had.

It was a cold January, but February promised a slight reprieve. Occasionally the sun would shine, and Jean was able to get the boys outside to play in the afternoon for an hour or two. They had just come in from one of their outdoor times and were all piled on her big double bed reading stories when Jean thought she heard a car door slam. She got up to see, and as she started down the short hallway, a knock came on the door.

Opening the door, Jean saw a man holding a white envelope. "Is this the Irwin's?"

Jean's heart almost stopped. The last time they had received a telegram, it had been announcing the death of Allan's father. Trembling, she opened it and read. WALTER PASSED STOP HEART ATTACK STOP FUNERAL SAT 2PM STOP LOVE GRACE.

Jean stumbled to a chair, sat down, and wept for poor, dear Grace. They had only been married 3 years. She dried her tears and wrote Grace a note of love and encouragement, stamped it and put it in the mailbox. It would go out today, and with any luck, she would get it in three days.

When Allan came home, he held her for a long time.

"Why do bad things happen to good people, Allan?"

He thought a while before answering. "Mother used to say that God was no respecter of persons and that His rain fell on the good as well as the bad. If this life is to be some kind of test, I reckon God has got to test the good right along with the bad."

Allan determined he would do an early milking Saturday, so they could leave to Grace's as soon as possible and stay as late as feasible.

It was a somber funeral as it always is for those who die before their time. Walter was just 62. Jean and Allan did their best to be of comfort to Grace. It was comforting just to have family there. She promised to come and stay with them for a week when she got her affairs in order. They had to leave in time to do the milking, and they left with heavy hearts.

Grace at home in White Rock.

Grace became a frequent visitor in their home over the next few months. She would stay and help Jean for a few days until the noise of the boys became too much even for her. Then she would catch the train back to Crescent Beach. On one of their trips to the train station, they approached a car turning left with a man holding his arm out to signal. In his hand, he held an ice-cream cone. As they passed, Allan reached out his window and made to grab the cone hollering, "Thank-you!" The motorist looked annoyed. Jean said, "Oh, Allan!" But Allan laughed and laughed! "Did you see the look on his face?"

Summer brought a flooded Silver Creek from the melted snow pack. Jean would often take the boys swimming there after morning chores were done. It was about a mile from their house at the bottom of Nelson Hill. Jean was an excellent swimmer and loved the cool water as much as the boys did. One day she sat on the bank changing John Bruce. He got away from her and, running down the bank, tripped and fell head first into twelve feet of water. Robin stood on the bank, watching him plunge down through the stream just like a little fish, the sunlight glistening on his tiny bare body. "Gee! I didn't know John could swim," he thought to himself. Jean was running right after him; she brushed by Robin, dove in, and pulled out a sputtering little boy.

The summer, as usual, brought the gardening and canning. The boys' growth necessitated a bigger garden and more canning. The big boys were, however, much more help to Jean. They could watch John Bruce and Lanny, hang out washing, churn butter, fill canning jars, fetch the wood, and bring an almost full bucket— sloshing with water— from the well. They also fed chickens, gathered eggs, and hauled water to the livestock. Allan would tell friends and family, "We have running water. Either Robin runs for it, or Ross runs for it!"

Ross would be starting school this fall; Jean was going to be busy sewing school clothes for two boys now. She could sometimes pass down the shirts but hardly ever a pair of pants. They never lasted in the knees. She longed for the day they could get electricity up their road and get an electric sewing machine. She would just have to make do with the old treadle machine for now.

Every so often Allan would take one of the three older boys on the milk run and point out things of interest to them. He pointed out the black and white Holsteins and the shaggy Highland cattle. He taught them how to cautiously approach a strange dog and that you approached most strange men that same way. Having just one of the boys away for the day provided a change of pace for Jean. It made being the mother of four rambunctious little fellows tolerable.

Sparky, Ross, Robin, Lanny, John Bruce, Allan and Buttons.

Allan would stop on occasion at the Silverdale gas station on a hot summer's day and buy gas and a cold bottle of pop for whichever of the boys was riding with him. The old fellow who owned the station commented on Robin's hat one day and then told Allan about a young high school age lad who had come in the store in the "dirty thirty's" wearing a brand new hat.

"There was a pot bellied stove in here in those days. One of the old timers who hung around the store asked the young fellow if he thought he could hit the same spot in the chopping block 3 times in a row with an axe while blindfolded. The young man was quite fond of himself and his abilities and said sure he could. A twenty-five-cent bet was made. Then a great to do ensued about removing the hat and getting the blindfold in place and the axe in hand. Well, when he took off that blindfold, the young fellow saw he had chopped his new hat in half!"

Robin stopped his pop bottle in mid–rise and stared at the man. Allan laughed.

Allan could not wait to get home and tell Jean the story. Robin hoped when his mother heard it she might let him stop wearing hats.

One afternoon Jean expected Jack's family to dinner. She had a big pot of rabbit stew cooking on the stove. Robin and Ross, trapped inside on a rainy afternoon, were chasing each other around the house when Robin knocked the pot of stew off the stove. It fell perfectly upside down on the linoleum floor. Grabbing a dinner plate Jean slipped it under the stew and flipped the pot right side up.

Glaring at the boys, she pointed an accusing finger and said, "If you so much as breathe one word about this to a single soul …!" There was no need to finish; the boys were terrified into silence. They ate their stew, like everyone else that night and thought it tasted just fine.

The truck drivers of the time were mostly veterans, like Allan. When they passed each other on the highway they would give a little ' V' sign, for victory, with their right hand on top of the steering wheel. Most of Allan's fellow workers were very polite and addressed each other as "Sir" as they would a superior in the military. One day however, when Allan had Robin with him at the milk plant, one of the drivers was regaling the others with ribald jokes. Allan took Robin and their lunch boxes and went far out of earshot. He did not want his boy picking up those stories.

Grace came out on the train to help Jean get the boys outfitted that last week before school. She had knitted them both Indian sweaters. They sewed up a storm; with Grace helping, one of them was always able to be on the treadle machine.

Finally, the opening day of school arrived with its usual last flurry of excitement. Jean and Grace loaded up all four boys to take them to Mission Central School by car. Jean did not want to send Ross by bus his first day. It was also the opening day of the brand new Mission Secondary School on 7th Avenue. Just as they were passing the entrance to the new High School, the school secretary, on a last minute errand, pulled up to the drive and, instead of hitting her brakes, stepped on the gas pedal. Her car sped across the street and plowed into the side of the family's Model A, flipping it over onto its side.

Inside the car Robin and Lanny had seen the vehicle speeding towards them and had both let out a terrific yell. When the car flipped over, the fabric headliner of the roof fell down and covered the little boys in the back seat. Ross began to feel decidedly claustrophobic and yelled, "I'm getting out of here!"

He began to kick savagely with his feet until he had kicked a hole in the fabric roof of the car. Other drivers stopped and pulled back on the roof, so Ross could crawl through feet first. Robin came right after him headfirst. Other motorists passing by helped drag Grace, Jean and the other two boys out of the car windows. John Bruce, who had just turned two, was screaming blue murder, but no one, miraculously, was seriously hurt. The car however was a total loss. A representative at the high school called a taxi for Jean, who, after depositing a slightly rumpled Ross and Robin at their school, took the others back to Nelson Road.

Jean crumpled in the rocker when she got home and had a good cry over their near miss but prayed in gratitude that none of her boys had been hurt or killed. John Bruce crawled into her lap, and Lanny came and stood next to her and laid his head on her arm. Grace bustled about the tiny kitchen to make a comforting cup of tea.

Allan was horrified when he arrived home that afternoon and heard the news. He walked down to meet the boys as they came home on the bus to make sure they were all right. He began right away to search for another car and found a 1933 dark blue Dodge four-door sedan. It was a six cylinder with hydraulic brakes. A stoic Grace returned home to Crescent Beach later that week on the train.

Late in September, Jean thought she must have caught the flu. She vomited for several days, but as no one else in the family had it, she began to wonder if she might be pregnant. She had never had morning sickness with any of the boys, but within a few weeks, there were other signs that she recognized. She found if she ate before getting up, it eased her stomach, so she kept a stash of Saltine crackers beside her bed.

The boys began preparing for Halloween in early October. They were all going to be cowboys as they already had the costumes. They begged to be allowed out alone, to trick or treat, like some of the older kids on the road, but Jean did not feel they were old enough yet. So while Jean kept John Bruce at home, Allan took the boys around the neighborhood, allowing them to walk up the long driveways by themselves. At the McNeal's, the boys were disappointed to get apples instead of candies, and on arriving home; they found the apples to be rotten.

Jean said "That's alright, boys, it was probably the best they had."

However, Robin and Ross were sure they had done it just to be mean and from that moment on began plotting their revenge.

By late in November Jean decided she had better go see Dr. Marcellus, and he confirmed that she was due in May.

Chapter 12

In 1953, Royalty came to Canada in the form of the young newly coroneted Queen Elizabeth, her husband Prince Phillip and their children, Prince Charles and Princess Anne. Their train traveled right through Mission. Nevertheless, Jean was too busy with the arrival of her own little princess to go down to the station to wave a flag. Her only daughter was born on May 18, weighing 7pounds 15 ounces. The boys all spent the days at Uncle Jack's with Auntie Edna watching them. When Allan got home from the hospital that first day, he ran down the road stopping at all the neighbors to tell them their family finally had a girl.

They named her Margaret Jean after both Jean's sister Margaret and Allan's sister, Margaret Grace. Allan loaded up all the boys to take them to pick up Jean and their new sister at the end of Jean's week in the hospital. Ross was seven at the time, and he remembers that he thought his Mum actually glowed when she came out to the car. Her eyes were certainly brimming over with tears. A nurse handed Jeannie into her mother's arms. All four boys stood up in the back and leaned over the front seat to get a glimpse of their new sister while Jean pulled the pink blanket back from her face.

John Bruce gave her a royal welcome to the family by saying, "Hey kid, do you want a fight?"

John Bruce and Jeannie 1953.

There was a major change in the dairy industry in 1953 that put the small producers like Allan out of business. It was the advent of the large refrigerated trucks and refrigerated facilities to store the milk at the farms before collection. Not only did it put the small farmers out of production, but it also put an end to the small trucks that collected. Allan was suddenly without work with a family of five kids to worry about. He sold all but two of his cows, which would see to their own personal needs. He was able to get part time work driving for Cannon Construction where Jack worked. It was enough to get by, but when that eventually ended and nothing else was available, he applied for unemployment insurance.

Weeks went by, but no check arrived. Jean prayed fervently that Allan would find work. Allan decided to go to the Member of Legislature over his Riding. His name was George Mussalem. He owned a General Motors Dealership in Haney. They told Allan at the constituency office that George was at the dealership. Allan showed up at the dealership and explained his problem to George. He invited Allan into his office, got hold of the department head in Victoria, and explained the problem. The department head informed Mr. Mussalem that the application was in the system and would be processed in due course. Mr. Mussalem advised the department head that was the wrong answer. He was a member of the B.C. Provincial Cabinet. He was going to stay on the line and wait until the department head came back on the phone with the right answer. A few minutes later, the gentleman came back on the line and said the check would be going out in that day's mail. Mr. Mussalem thanked the man for his help and hung up the phone. Allan was most appreciative, and George just smiled and said he was happy he could be of some service.

Lanny, Ross, Robin holding Jeannie and John Bruce.

It was difficult for Allan to find a new job; he was 51 years old and knew farming and truck driving. He bought a few calves and found some success at fattening them up over the summer and selling them for beef in the fall. Jack helped him butcher one of the steers for their own use, and they cut and wrapped all the meat in white butcher paper and stored it at Frankie's Locker in town.

He sold firewood, door to door, and sold sand to the Department of Highways from his huge sandpit at the edge of the big hill. They were just barely able to scrape by.

He had the pony, Star, bred with a Shetland pony, and she gave birth to a tiny, brown filly they named Buttons for a round, white spot on her nose. So there were two girls born on the farm that year, a fact that Jean often pointed out in later years to give comfort to little, sadly outnumbered, Jeannie.

One day, while in town, Allan happened to run into "Flying Phil" Giglardi, a member of Premier Bennett's Cabinet. As Minister of Highways, he was a powerful and influential fellow. He had received the moniker "Flying Phil" because he was frequently stopped for speeding. He would reportedly say to the unwitting officer, "Do you know who I am? I'm Phil Giglardi, and it's my job to make sure the highways are safe!"

He asked Allan how he was doing.

"Not very well," Allan replied. "I have five kids and no job." Two weeks later Allan had the offer of a truck-driving job with the Department of Highways. He would stay at that until he retired at sixty-five.

Lanny, Robin, Jeannie, Jean, Ross and John Bruce on their one upholstered chair.

Grace left that summer to return to Manitoba. She, like Allan, missed the wide-open blue prairie sky. She spent some time with her sister, Bella, and Bella's husband Mac in Wawanessa and then settled into a home of her own.

Grandma Peebles wrote to invite the boys up to the log house in Tulameen for two weeks at the end of the summer. So Jean took the boys, Robin, nine, Ross, seven, and Lanny, six, to the train station and bought them tickets for the one hundred and sixty-mile trip to Tulameen. Jean's father had worked on the Canadian Pacific Railway until retirement, and Jean knew many of the people who worked the train route through the

Coquihalla. She trusted that they would watch over her boys. The porters were all of African heritage, and they were the first black people the boys had ever seen. One of the porters, a huge man, came lumbering down the platform towards them and called out, "Hello there, Jean!"

The boys stared at their mother in amazement. To think their own mother could be acquainted with such exotic people.

Jean entrusted Ross to carry a small silver donkey brooch, wrapped in white tissue paper, in his pocket as a gift for Grandma. Ross was immensely proud that she had chosen him for this honor. The huge porter told Jean before the train pulled out, "Don't you worry any about your boys, Jean. I'll see they get off in Tulameen."

The train traveled at night. The view over the cliff sides was so scary the railway owners figured if the people could actually see where they were, they would have no repeat customers. There was not much for the boys to see except the lights of the little communities they passed – places named by a Shakespeare enthusiast- Othello, Lear, Iago, even Romeo, and Juliet.

The only major excitement was the noisy passing of another train in the middle of the night and waving to its passengers. They found out years later there was only one track through the Coquihalla Mountains. It was their own train, passing over switchbacks, to which they had waved.

At Tulameen, the boys stayed in the bunkhouse at night with their cousins, Johnny, Stan, Bud, and Rick. The bunkhouse was just a smaller log cabin where their uncles had lived while building the log house. It was quite a distance from the house and dark as pitch. Robin was in ghost story heaven! Occasionally, they would hear an animal crashing through the dense woods during the night, and that was enough to scare even Robin silly.

There was a potbelly stove in the cabin, but, as it was summer while the boys were there, it was never lit. There was a box of matches on the shelf over the stove and the claim printed on the side of the box read "NO AFTERGLOW." One night, Johnny lit one of these matches in the dark of the cabin and, holding it up for all the boys to see, blew out the flame. The boys all watched that little pinprick of light glow in the absolute darkness. Johnny, waxing poetic, called out in a singsong voice, "I fooled you. I fooled you. There's afterglow inside of you." For years afterward, the boys repeated that little ditty whenever they fooled each other.

Grandma's log house was full of wonders for the boys. It had a rock fireplace where they could enjoy the novelty of sitting around an indoor fire. It had hot running water and a real bathtub as opposed to their own tin tub at home. It had stairs down to a deliciously scary basement. They would get halfway down the stairs before fear overcame them, and they would come running up and slam the door behind them. Grandma was quite strict and soon put a stop to that nonsense.

Outdoors was a wonderland, miles of pine forest and the Tulameen River just a short walk from the house. They built a wonderful fort in the woods close to the house. Grandma would not let them out of earshot, as there were bears in the woods. She and Grandpa would take them swimming at the river in the Dredge hole.

The Dredge hole was a result of long ago gold mining, by machine, on the river. On one such outing as they headed down the steep driveway, they thought they heard a baby crying. They all stopped and listened. The boys determined it was in the woods at the bottom of the drive and wanted to go and get it but Grandma said, "Just stand *still*!" The boys waited impatiently while the crying continued. Presently a young black bear cub came out of the bushes, bawling, and headed up the road toward them.

"Never get between a cub and his mother," Grandma warned.

"Wouldn't it be funny," Robin stated with a chuckle, "if we turned around, and the mother bear was right behind us!" They looked at one another, then they all turned around slowly, and there she was, coming out of the woods at the top of the drive and lumbering down towards them.

"Move slowly, nobody run!" calmly instructed Grandma.

She and the boys moved directly sideways to the shelter of the basement porch and watched the bereft cub reunite with his mother and ramble off into the woods. The boys carried their stick guns at the ready from then on.

When they reached the swimming hole, Grandma sat on a blanket in the shade out of the blistering sun. The boys were already splashing around in the Dredge hole, but Lanny stood on the bank with just his feet in the glacier fed river. He was going to take his time easing into it. Three brothers, local Indian boys from Tulameen were also there today. They swam in the buff. The youngest one, who was about Lanny's age, came out and stood on the bank close by where Lanny was easing in. The youngster had taken enough of his brothers teasing.

"Come on Luke. Come on back in. We won't splash you anymore."

Luke shook his head. Lanny heard a buzzing over the roar of the river and lazily turned his head to watch a large bumblebee dancing about in the searing air. He watched it approach the boy but Luke, his gaze fixed on his brothers, paid no attention to it. The local boys had resorted to splashing Robin, Ross, and the cousins who splashed back with vigor. Lanny continued to watch the bee as it darted about the boy and then suddenly landed. He was just about to shout a warning when Luke let out a blood-curdling scream and, grabbing his privates, began hopping frantically from one foot to the other. The boys all stopped their splashing and stared at him.

"What happened?" one of his brothers called.

Lanny shouted back, "He got stung by a bee!"

Luke's brothers hurriedly waded to shore and, restraining him, looked at his injury. One brother said, "You're going to have to go to the hospital with that."

"Yeah," the other brother expounded, "they're going to have to amputate!"

Luke looked at them in horror then turned and ran bare foot and naked down the gravel road toward Tulameen screaming at the top of his lungs. The bigger boys all laughed hysterically. Lanny walked gingerly over the hot river boulders and sat on the blanket beside Grandma.

The boys at the dredge hole-Tulameen River.

All too soon, the boy's vacation was over, and they had another exciting ride home on the train. A staggering drunk approached them on the train. Ross and Lanny scooted over on the seat as far away from him as possible. Their eyes got big and round, and they did not breathe a word, but Robin chatted away as if he was their long lost uncle. The watchful porters probably thought he was! They were welcomed at the Mission station by their happy parents, relieved to have them safely home.

Lanny started school that fall and his teacher, not knowing differently, called him by his given name, Allan. The name stuck, and eventually his siblings adopted it, but his parents always called him Lanny.

Allan Sr. stopped in on occasion to check on Ernie Nelson. One afternoon Ernie invited him in for coffee. Allan was startled to see a huge pile of empty tin cans mounded beside the kitchen table. He tried not to stare, but he was sure he could hear faint rustling noises emanating from it. Sure enough, a movement caught his eye, and a little brown mouse, his whiskers all-aquiver, peered out at him. Ernie rapped his spoon on the table, and the mouse darted back under cover. Allan carefully averted his eyes from the pile and picking up his coffee cup slowly, took a drink. The silence stretched uncomfortably around them as thick as the dark brew they were drinking. He had heard rumors in previous years, on the milk run, of this pet mouse that ate right out of Ernie's hand.

Unexpectedly, Ernie came to the rescue. "That is a very interesting dog you have!"

"Oh yeah, why is that?"

"Well, I see him come running through my woods every morning, so I followed him one day to see what he was up to. He sits at the top of my hill and watches those kids of yours get on the school bus. Then when the bus leaves, he turns around and runs back home. Every day it's the same thing!"

Allan laughed, "Jean was just saying to me she swears that dog can tell time! He goes and sits by the road every day at 3 o'clock. Then when he hears the bus stop, he runs down to walk home with the kids. Animals sure are puzzlement sometimes."

Keeping his eyes averted from the pile of tin cans, Allan managed to take another swallow of his coffee.

That fall the boys were deemed responsible enough to go around by themselves for Halloween. This fit perfectly with their plans. They had been plotting revenge on the McNeal's for the rotten apples all year long. In Canada, firecrackers were sold at Halloween until they were outlawed, the authorities determining that the combination of little kids in the dark handling explosives was somehow lethal. The Nelson Road Gang always managed to have firecrackers at Halloween. This year, with them still being legal, they had hold of a half dozen six-inch "bombs." These, combined with several paper hand-soap boxes hidden downstairs in the basement, formed the basis of the boys' plan.

Finally, dusk arrived, and the three boys, appropriately costumed, were out the door. Retrieving the paper soapboxes, they excitedly headed off to get revenge. Halfway there, they packed the bombs in the boxes with dirt and small rocks. Giddy with excitement they ran down the dark road to their target. Stealthily, they approached the house, placed the "bombs" on the front porch, lit the fuses and ran for cover. The bombs exploded, scattering dirt across the porch and against the front window. To the boys delight, they heard a scream and a holler from inside the house.

As Mr. McNeal heatedly told Allan later that night, they thought someone was shooting at their window, and Mrs. McNeal had nearly had a heart attack. Though they were not spanked on many occasions, the boys certainly "had earned it this time." They were also made, with their sore bottoms, to march down to the offended neighbors and apologize.

Chapter 13

1954

The family's favorite section of *The Vancouver Sun* was the funny pages. Everyone had to have their own turn to look at it whether they could read yet or not. The boys often fought over who was going to get it first. One of their favorite comic strips was "Pogo." He was a sarcastic little opossum whose adventures sometimes involved a homemade raft. Perhaps the comic strip was their inspiration or perhaps it was because that spring every nook and hollow was awash with rainwater. Whatever the motivation, the boys decided it was a genius idea to build a raft. They raided Allan's construction woodpile and built a sizable scow with 2x2's for a frame and ¼-inch plywood for the deck. They christened it "Pogo" and proceeded to drag the heavy craft to the largest available body of water, a pond deep in a neighbor's woods, about a quarter mile from the house.

Not sure if their raft would float, Robin uncharacteristically appointed the lightest brother to take it out on its maiden voyage. Thus, Lanny, to his great surprise, was allowed to take the first turn. He climbed aboard the unsteady vessel, and Robin and Ross launched it with a mighty shove. About 25 feet from shore, "Pogo" began to take on water. Lanny understandably panicked and stood up. The raft capsized and Lanny, without other options, found himself floundering around in waist deep water that was colder than a mother-in-laws heart. He stumbled to shore yelling at his older brothers that the water was *really* cold and that they were idiots! Robin and Ross, extremely concerned they would miss their turns, hollered frantically, "Bring the boat. Bring the boat!" Lanny did not give "Pogo" a second thought but ran straight for home.

Jean stripped him out of his soaking wet clothes, rubbed the shivering boy down with a rough towel, wrapped him in a quilt, and set him in a chair beside the wood stove. When his teeth stopped chattering, he was able to give his account of the launch and subsequent sinking of "Pogo." Jean frowned and shook her head. Unable to retrieve their sunken vessel, his brothers dejectedly returned home. When Allan arrived home, he warmed up both their behinds for coming up with such a risky idea. Jean was just thankful they lived as far away from the Fraser River as they did.

Lanny, John Bruce, Jean holding Jeannie, Ross, Robin and Sparky.

With the three older boys now in school, Jean enlisted John Bruce to help with farm chores. At four, Jean thought him old enough to help feed the chickens and gather their eggs.

Unfortunately, the chicken coop was lorded over by a large, possessive red rooster. On Johns' first day of doing the chore all by himself, the rooster let out a tremendous cock-a–doodle-do, flew down from his post atop the coop, and chased after the little fellow, pecking at his legs. John ran screaming for the house and, from that day on, was scared of chickens in general and roosters in particular for many years to come.

Grace had mentioned in her letters that she had a gentleman friend, but it still was a surprise to receive her letter announcing her wedding date to Jimmy Nicholson for the 23 of March 1954. Jean wrote back right away demanding to know all about Grace's Jimmy. It would be years before they could actually meet him. However, when they finally did, Allan pronounced him "a fine fellow!"

With a steady job and a growing family, Allan began to think of adding on to the house. One day he asked Jean to go for a walk with him. Taking her by the hand and climbing to the top of the small hill, he proceeded to point out how level the top of it was, how far from the dust of the road it would be and the great view it afforded. Then he dropped the bombshell.

"What would you think if I moved the house up here?"

Stunned, she queried, "You want to move the house? However would you do it?"

"Well I'm not sure, Jean. Maybe I could jack it up, put poles under it, and tow it with the truck. I am sure it can be done somehow. I want to dig a proper basement and add a living room and some more bedrooms. I still have lots of building material from that old church. There's a gentle slope to that ravine that comes up the back of the hill. I can clear a road up that way."

She shook her head in amazement!

"Well, if you think you can do it, I suppose there is no stopping you," she said with a half hearted smile.

They planned where the house site would be, and Allan took note of the trees he would have to take down. Jean returned to the house, and Allan got started right away. It would take him several years to complete the project.

One weekend Allan took Robin and Ross on a wood delivery run to a fellow employee at the highway department. When the wood was unloaded, the chap invited, "Come on out back and see the shed I built."

It was a nice shed with racks, hangers and every imaginable kind of tool, all painted orange. On the drive home, the boys were exclaiming over his wonderful shop and Robin asked his Dad, "wouldn't you like to have a shop like that?"

The boys were puzzled by Allan's gruff reply. "Too much darned orange paint for my taste."

It was not until many years later, when Robin worked a short time for the Department of Highways that he understood his Dad's irritation. All the tools in the department were painted bright orange or at least had a band of orange paint around the handle.

The highways department was all new territory for Allan's tricks. One day at work, he spotted a wild brown bunny and, with a little patience, was able to catch it. As it was close to a coffee break, he put the bunny into an unsuspecting co-worker's metal lunch pail after taking out the fellow's sandwiches. The trap set, the crew chief called everyone over for an early coffee break. They all sat down on the side of the road, and Allan's victim popped open his lunch box. The rabbit, pretty agitated by this time, leaped out onto the fellows lap, scaring him out of his wits. He jumped up yelling and swearing and kicked his lunch box out into the highway, breaking his thermos in the process.

Another day while driving truck, Allan had a fellow worker as a passenger. After dumping his load of gravel and preparing to turn the truck, he realized his passenger was sound asleep. Pulling up to the very edge of an embankment, he set the brake then gunned the engine, honked the horn and shouted, "Jump! Jump! We're going over!" His co-worker woke up in a fright, saw the traffic whizzing by on the highway below them, jumped out and went head over heels down the bank. Fortunately, there was a good wide ditch for him to land in.

One day after work, Allan showed up at the house with a highways department truck full of fence posts. He had started to unload them by the barn when Jean came out of the house to see what was going on. Just then, Allan's foreman showed up.

"I just thought I should come by and tell you, Mrs. Irwin, that Allan has permission to use the truck, and we were just going to burn the fence posts anyway."

He knew Allan was completely honest but thought it best to come reassure Jean on that fact.

Later that year while driving home from a visit to Jack's, the family's car was hit head on by a drunk driver. Little Jeannie, not yet two, was torn from her mother's arms and thrown against the windshield, putting deep gashes in her hairline and above her right eyebrow. Concerned motorists got the family to the hospital, and Jeannie was soon stitched back together. Not as easily fixed, the car was declared totaled. It was some time before a suitable replacement could be found, and so for a time they made do with the old Dodge flatbed truck.

The beat up old Dodge truck was less than desirable transportation. Allan made a box on the back where the three oldest boys could sit. John Bruce and Jeannie rode with their parents up front on the bench seat.

Jean had determined that the family was going to attend church. Allan looked fine all dressed in his dark blue pin striped suit, and Jean was beautiful when dressed up in her light blue dotted Swiss dress. She always dressed the children well when going out anywhere in shirts, ties, and hats. That first Sunday they appeared at the _____ Church in Mission, the clergyman who was quite pleased to see a fine looking new family in his congregation met them at the door. He welcomed them with gushing enthusiasm. The following Sunday they were lucky enough to find a parking spot right by the front door. Allan watched the look on the clergyman's face as he unloaded his family from that beat up old truck. That day they were met with much less enthusiasm and Allan did not darken the door of that building ever again.

Back row: Ross, Robin and Lanny. Front row: Allan, Bruce, Jeannie and Jean.

Surrounded, as they were on the farm, by horses, cows and thick woods, the boys would naturally play a lot of Cowboys and Indians. They had an old tin basin of Jean's and a green rag that gave off plenty of dye, which was the cure for bullet wounds and arrowheads. If you were shot, one swipe of that green dye, and you were back in the game.

One of the indispensible props in their play was "the hanging tree." Robin was a consummate storyteller, and the large cedar just to the east of the house was where all the bad guys from their cowboy games were hung, hence the name. This tree was not to be confused with "dead mans tree", another ridiculously large cedar at the far east of the property line. This apparently

114

received its name because if you fell out of it, you were definitely a dead man.

Chapter 14

1955

Their own car totaled, Allan decided for their New Year's celebration at Jack's, he would borrow a car from Wally Little. The highlight of this year's party was making ice cream. Jean and Allan had brought the heavy cream that was placed, with sugar, in a steel-lidded container with a hand crank, similar to a butter churn. This, however, had an outer wooden pail that held chipped ice and rock salt, which increased the coldness of the ice. What a treat!

"My ice cream is too cold," Ross insisted. "Can we heat it up in the oven?"

After spending the evening with Jack's family up on Tunbridge Road, they commenced the drive home. Headed down Cedar Valley Road, at a sharp decline, they could see a stalled car in their lane at the bottom of the ravine. Pulled in front of it was another car, and the two drivers were between the cars attaching a towrope. Compounding the traffic jam was a third car headed up the hill in the opposite lane whose driver had stopped to chat with the other two drivers. As Allan attempted to slow down, he suddenly realized he had no brakes! There was a cryptic exchange between Jean and Allan. Allan expressed his dissatisfaction with the mental abilities of the driver coming up hill, blocking their only escape route and Jean reminded him he was not to talk like that in front of the children. Having already been in two serious crashes, the children were all acutely aware of the possibilities.

"Hang on," Allan said. "If nobody moves we may be ok."

Taking the only other option available, Allan swerved to pass to the right of the stalled car on the gravel shoulder. The problem with this was the sharp drop off and a deep water reservoir to the right. From Jean's vantage point in the front right hand seat, holding Jeannie, and Robin's in the back right hand seat, it appeared they sailed past those cars on their two left wheels. All they could see under the running board was the water of the reservoir. Robin thought if they somehow managed to survive, he was going to have a great story to tell at school on Monday.

Luckily, the stalled car and their own had no side mirrors. There was a lot of screaming and cursing by the two men in between the two cars. The driver, who had stopped to chat, began honking his horn frantically. However, of course, there was no stopping to explain their actions, and they limped slowly on home to Nelson Road.

As Allan later said, "If the paint had been a little thicker, we wouldn't have made it."

Allan visited all the local car dealerships in the close vicinity to let them know he was looking for a good used car. The next Saturday morning, the family was all out working in the garden when Mr. Ross Coleman came driving up to the house. He owned the GM dealership in Mission and was an impeccable dresser and handsome as could be. The car he had brought to show Allan had belonged to his father, Old Mr. Coleman. It was a 1941 Chevy, burgundy-wine in color, with more chrome than the boys had ever seen, and though it was fourteen years old, it ran smooth as silk. Allan signed the papers there in the yard and then went back into town with Mr. Coleman to bring the car home.

It proved to be a great car, especially in the winter. Allan kept some weight in the trunk, but his real secret weapon was a set of Sears Suburbanite Winter tires. They would take him any where in any weather, and they lasted for years. He came home one day from a trip to town completely disgusted that he was unable to buy another set of those tires.

"The salesman told me they were discontinued because they took too long to wear out!"

Allan had a dream of starting a pony farm. Star and her filly, Buttons, were the smaller classic British style Shetland ponies. The slightly larger American style Shetland's were derived from breeding Arab horses, Welsh, and Shetland ponies. The result was a Shetland that looked more like a small horse than a plush toy.

When Allan decided to get a stallion for breeding, Whidbey Island in Washington State was determined to be the closest source. Robin, Ross, and Lanny were selected to go on this great adventure with their Dad.

One of the outstanding features of Whidbey Island is Deception Pass Bridge. The bridge is actually two bridges divided, about a quarter of the way across the span, by a great tall rock called Pass Island. There is a flat area with parking spaces for visitors, and Allan stopped the car to let the kids stretch their legs after the long, three-hour drive. The boys immediately took off running with Robin in the lead.

The most common of all cries, in all families with more than one child is, "Wait for me." This family was no exception. With his two younger brothers coming on as hard as they could behind him, hollering for him to wait, Robin, uncharacteristically, paused in his headlong rush and waited for them to catch up. He put his foot on the handy log in front of him and saw, just off the toe of his shoe, what appeared to be a tiny toy boat with little tiny toy people fishing off the deck surrounded by very realistic looking water. Robin held out his arm and yelled at his brothers to stop and pushing aside the little huckleberry bush in front of them, solemnly looked down a hundred and eighty feet of empty air to the water below. They would have nightmares of this instant in time for years to come.

The pony farm was about ten acres divided into one acre paddocks. When the farmer rattled some grain in a bucket, the ponies all came storming up the slope towards them with manes and tails flying, the young colts and fillies gamboling along with reckless abandon. The mares all raced to be first to receive the promised grain. The boys thought they had died and gone to cowboy heaven! They all agreed the most handsome of the stallions was a copper/gold pony with a white mane and tail, named Chester, out of Bright Penny. Allan had built a wooden box in the back seat of the 41 Chevy to level out the floor, so they could bring the pony home. Chester stood in this box with his head stuck out the open window.

While stopped at a red light in Bellingham, Washington, Chester let out a real trumpet solo of a whinny that caused two middle aged ladies to stumble all over themselves and a young African American man to look startled enough to near have a heart attack.

"My goodness, boys, you would think he never saw a horse riding in a car before." Allan chucked the rest of the way home.

The next day Allan lined up all three ponies, Star, Buttons, and Chester, to take pictures of them with the kids. Jeannie, in the middle of the process, started screaming and could not be consoled. A week later, when they got the pictures back, it appeared that in one of them Buttons was biting Jeannie's arm. They pulled up the sleeve of her blouse, and sure enough, the teeth marks were still there.

Buttons biting Jeannie.

The boys were rarely allowed to sleep in. Allan would wake them up by singing in his loud tenor, "Oh it's nice to get up in the morning when the sun begins to shine, five or six or seven o clock in the good ole summertime. But when it's kind of cloudy and its murky overhead, well, it's nice to get up in the morning, but I'd rather stay in bed!"

On Saturdays, the boys helped their Dad with logging the property among other chores. Robin learned to drive the old 31 Dodge truck by the time he was old enough to reach the pedals, at 11. Allan had rigged a pulley arrangement to pull logs out of the gully. He would drive the truck to the top of the hill and turn it around to face downhill. He would then have Robin slide over to the driver's seat, and he would jump down and hook a log to the cable. The truck had hydraulic brakes, and they usually worked well, but like all hydraulic systems, they will leak and then require repair. It was, however, possible to operate the truck, if they were careful, without any brakes, which they did for a week or so on the log pull that year. They just had to be very quick with the shift so that they could hold the truck in place on the hill with the clutch while the cable was hooked on. One day when Robin was driving, he missed the shift, and the truck started rolling downhill. Without the attached weight of the log, it naturally got rolling a lot faster than normal.

Allan came running behind the truck hollering, "Put on the brakes!"

Robin thought, "That's real stupid. The truck has not had brakes for at least a week."

Again, Allan yelled, "Put on the brakes!"

The truck was gathering speed, and Robin was afraid he was going to tear out a couple of fences and end up out on Nelson Road. He looked frantically for another option. Just beyond the bottom of the hill was a tremendous big stump. Robin aimed for it, thinking if he hit it with the frame end; it would not damage the truck and would certainly stop it.

He aimed for the stump while still hearing his Dad yelling. "Put on the brakes!" There was a loud bang, and the truck shuddered to a halt.

Allan was to the truck in a minute and threw open the door. "Why didn't you use the brakes, you darn fool?" he yelled.

Robin yelled right back, "You darn fool, it has no brakes!"

"Well," Allan said only slightly apologetically, "I fixed the brakes while you were at school yesterday."

Robin felt like an idiot, but he also felt that Dad should have mentioned that minor fact before he got in the truck.

John Bruce was only five that September, so he had to wait another year to start school. He was eager to learn anything the boys would teach him. One night as they lay whispering and giggling in bed, Allan yelled at them to quiet down and get to sleep.

Bruce hollered right back, "One and one makes two. I can say as much as you. Two and two makes four. Shut your mouth, and say no more!"

That was one 5 year old who got a licking for something he had learned "from school."

Sparky, John Bruce and Jeannie.

One of the boy's regular games was tree riding. They would climb to the top of a spindly vine maple and get it swaying back and forth, often touching right to the ground and pushing off with their feet. Lanny was riding a less flexible Cedar one day when the tree snapped and he fell, unbroken but winded, about ten feet to the ground.

He was not nearly so lucky when he fell while playing in the hayloft. The hay was loosely stacked in three levels, like steps, and the boys would start at the top and, with a holler, roll or jump or slide to the lowest level. One day Lanny rolled right off the end of the lowest level and, falling to the ground heard a sickening snap. The pain made him nauseas. A neighbor boy, Alan Varga, was very concerned when he heard Lanny had broken his arm and, in all sincerity, asked, "Did they find it?"

Allan had completely cleared the roadbed and site for the house that year and started working to dig out, by hand, the basement for the house. The footprint of the house was to be a little over twice the size of the existing home with a bedroom in the attic for two of the boys, a living room, a new bedroom for Jean and Allan and a bedroom of her own for Jeannie. Jean and Allan's current bedroom would become a laundry room.

Allan purchased Jean an oil cook stove in the fall, which was far more convenient. A cheerful fellow, by the name of Elmer _____, who was a neighbor and good friend of Jack's, delivered the oil. Jeannie and John Bruce were often outside, dressed in their older brothers' hand-me-down snowsuits with hoods, and Elmer would tease, "How are you doing, *boys*?" Jeannie would always stomp her foot and answer indignantly, "I am a *girl*!"

Elmer worked for the Home Oil bulk plant. Allan would ask for purple gas delivered which was available only to farmers for off-road use. It was cheaper as it had no tax added. Allan had his own 45-gallon drum for the gas. Elmer would fill the drum and then give Allan the package of purple dye to put in, saying, "Put this in, Al, while I do the paperwork."

Consequently, Allan's pickup truck often ran on tax-free gas while there was no danger of a police officer finding his carburetor stained purple, as he never put the dye in the drum.

That Christmas Grace sent presents for all the kids from Manitoba. The most memorable was a plump stuffed doll that she had fashioned for Jeannie. Made of a soft blue cotton fabric and filled with foam, it had a round cream-colored face with embroidered eyes, nose, and mouth. Jeannie adored it! When asked what her new babies name was, she thought of the other thing she loved the most and answered, "Pie."

The boys hooted and laughed at such a silly name, but Jean said, "It's a perfect name for her!"

Jeannie smiled smugly at the boys.

Chapter 15

1956

Ross heard at school that *The Vancouver Sun* paper route on Nelson Road was going to be available as a walking route. There were enough new people on the road to warrant the change. He convinced Jean and Allan that he was responsible enough, so they let him take the job. He picked up his papers, a short walk out to the highway from the bus stop, at a big orange wooden box that had *Vancouver Sun* painted on the top. His whole route was 4-5 miles long. There were seven customers, and he earned about $3.50 a month. It took him several years to save enough to buy a bike.

The paperboys were also responsible for collecting customer's money each month; it was the worst part of the job. One of the customers, Mr. S_____, would always ask Ross if he had change for a twenty. As he never did, the man would ask him to come back another day. Ross eventually complained to his Dad about the stingy customer.

"Whether you have the change or not, tell him that you do." Allan advised his son.

The next time the man pulled this trick, Ross said he had change. The man stared at him a moment and then handed him two one dollar bills and fifty cents. It was the last time he had a problem with that customer.

Another of the customers, Mr. M_____, would always be out working when Ross went to collect. Ross would have to traipse around the farm to locate him. He would tell the boy to wait a minute, go into the barn, and come back with the money.

Ross thought it strange for him to keep his money in the barn, so one month while collecting, he peered through a crack in the barn wall. The farmer shucked off his coat, undid his coveralls, and pulled them down. Reaching into the pocket of a second pair of pants, he pulled out a huge wad of bills and peeled off three.

Later that night, Ross asked his Dad, "Why doesn't Mr.M____ take all that money to the bank?"

"Some people, who lived through the depression years, just don't trust the banks anymore. They keep their money in cash at home."

It was another dry summer. Their well could barely keep up with their needs for water in the house let alone take care of all the livestock. Allan determined to dig their 25-foot well a little deeper. He climbed down the wooden cribbing of the side of the well, dug a bucket full of earth, and hollered at the boys to haul it up with a pulley, rigged over the well, and dump it.

One day Ross made the mistake of looking down as his Dad was climbing back out. Allan had stopped to rest about 15 feet from the top. Ross gulped and broke out in a sweat. He was sure his Dad was going to fall. It made him feel so sick he sat down on the ground with his back against the well and put his head between his knees. Allan found him there a few minutes later.

"You O.K., son?"

Ross just nodded and heaved himself to his feet.

Electricity was available up the road that year, and Jean was ecstatic! They unearthed their radio and purchased a sewing machine. The treadle machine was permanently stowed inside its table, and the electric machine sat proudly on top. Wednesdays night was the boys' night to listen to radio shows. Their favorites were *B Bar B Ranch*, *The Goon Show,* and *The Shadow.*

They drove all the way to New Westminster to purchase a refrigerator. It was a "Leonard" brand (proclaimed in silver letters on the door), and the boys took to calling it Leonard like it was a new member of the family. One of them would say, "I wonder what Leonard would say about that?", and the others would laugh.

They loved the fact that Leonard kept the milk cold: it was an unusual luxury.

Jean would bathe the children, until they got too big to lift, in the kitchen sink. It was easier than filling the tub. She had bathed Jeannie one night and then set her down on a pile of newspaper beside the sink. When she stood her up again, one of the boys pointed and laughed, and then all the boys began laughing. She had comic strips printed across her wet behind. Jeannie began screaming with embarrassment.

Meanwhile Allan kept busy on the new home site. He had purchased a Fresno Scraper, a walk behind, horse drawn scoop, with two handles much like a wheelbarrow without the wheel. It had a big metal hoop in the front where the horse, Jess, was hitched. He had used this to dig a road down the side of the gully. However, he later switched to Jean driving the truck and pulling the scoop as it was so much more efficient. By this means, he dug four trenches the depth of the new basement. When these were finally dug, he built wooden forms and poured them full of cement to create the basement walls. The cement he made from purchased gravel mixed with sand he hauled, with the truck, from their sandpit.

The trench created a fantastic place to scare younger siblings and all the little neighborhood kids. Robin and Ross hooked up an old white sheet on a clothesline and then led kids through the trench looking for ghosts. One of them would be hidden in the dark and send the sheet flying down the trench towards the terrified spectators all the while screaming like a banshee. The little adventurers would fall all over each other trying to escape and scream with delighted terror.

Old friends of Allan's dropped by that summer on a visit to the coast from Russell, Manitoba. Jean and Allan were delighted to show them around their farm. Jeannie, age 3, thought it would be terribly funny to impress the company. While everyone was at the corral meeting the ponies, she slipped into the tack shack, took off all her clothes, climbed in a gunnysack and hopped out in front of the group. Jean's face was indescribable. She took one look and hollered, "Jeannie!"

Jeannie knew by the tone she was in trouble. She dropped the sack where she stood and made a run for the shack, chased by a roar of laughter. Having shown more than she planned, she did not dare to show her face until the company was long gone.

Jeannie.

John Bruce turned six that summer and started school with his brothers. His teacher, also not knowing any better than Lanny's teacher, shortened his name to John. Jeannie, left at home without any of the boys to play with, had to invent things to do. She loved to build forts with chairs placed back to back and a blanket roof draped over top.

Jean would sometimes leave her in the house alone while she ran out to check on the livestock. Jeannie realized that this was a good time for exploring, and her favorite spot was the forbidden top drawer of her parent's dresser. Standing on the edge of the bed, she was just barely able to pull open the heavy brown wooden drawer. It was filled with breakable statues

Jean had hidden away for safekeeping. Jeannie loved to look at the glass birds, animals, and elves. There were perfume bottles and jewelry, and this particular day, Jeannie opened a black box about 4 inches square. She discovered it contained broken jewelry, and the piece that caught her eye was gold, shiny, and stretchy. She did not know it was a watchband. It looked like a short necklace to her, and so she stretched it out and put it around her neck. When she let go, all those sharp little teeth closed around the tender skin of her neck. Not having sense enough to stretch it to get it off, she left it on, stood stock still and started screaming at the top of her lungs.

Jeannie feeding the chickens.

Jean heard her all the way from the barn and came running frantically to the house. She removed the offending watchband, and Jeannie received no other punishment except the sore, red neck and being called a "silly little goose."

It had been pouring during the night, but the sun was working hard to peep through in the morning. Jean had dressed Jeannie in her Sunday best and, with constant prodding, was encouraging the boys to finish dressing and get out to the car. Allan would not go with them to church, but there was no way she was going to be responsible for raising a tribe of little heathens. Jeannie wandered outside, intending to wait in the car but there was no one to open the car door for her yet. It was then she saw the size of the puddles in the yard. She toddled over and wondered how deep the muddy water was. Carefully she set in one patent leather foot. The water did not even cover her shoe. She was halfway across the largest puddle when John Bruce came out of the house. He watched her for just a second before shouting, "You're really going to get it!"

"Get what?"

"A spanking."

She snorted in reply. "What was he talking about?" she thought to herself, "Only boys get spankings."

John Bruce went back inside. She turned away from the house and sloshed her way across the huge puddle for the second time. Suddenly, she felt someone grab her arm, lift her right out of the water, and at the same time administer a sound slap on her behind. She looked up in surprise to find her mother scowling down at her. She was so startled; she forgot to cry until she saw John Bruce grinning at her from the back step. Then she let out an inconsolable wail

132

Leaving the boys at home, Jean and Allan took Jeannie on an errand to town with them. Silver Creek, at the bottom of Nelson Hill, was running high, and the water was a good three inches over the top of the bridge deck. Allan stopped the car and got out to take a good look at the situation. He came back to the car and was all for proceeding over the bridge.

"Let's go around the other way," Jean suggested.

"No, it will be fine," Allan said.

Jeannie jumped up, leaned over the seat, and piped up, "I want to go the other way."

Allan told her to be quiet, put the car in gear and headed over. Jeannie lay down on the back seat, so she could not see the water. But, as fate would have it, the car had rusty floorboards, and there was a hole clear through the bottom. She could see the creek rushing by underneath the car. She was too terrified to make a sound. Thankfully, Jean convinced Allan to go home the other way, via the highway, and they were spared another crossing of the flooded bridge. However, the damage done, Jeannie would be terrified of deep water for the rest of her life.

Silver creek flooded. Jeannie in foreground bridge in background.

Chapter 16

By 1957, everything was in place to begin moving the house to its new site on the hilltop. A roadway and a building site had been cleared. The cement foundation was poured, and all the lumber moved to the site for the addition. A moving company jacked up the house and placed a wheeled frame under it.

The family took temporary shelter in a long unused berry pickers shed on the Bodners' property just down the road a piece from their own place. It was an exciting move for all the kids, being directly across the road from their friends, the Littles, and a recently arrived family the Bruckals. They could play late with their friends until Mummy called them in for dinner and were a slightly closer walk to the bus stop.

Jeannie, Terri Bruckal, Sparky, and Myles Bruckal.

A lot closer to Mr. Nelson's farm they were able to do more exploring in his dense woods. One day the boy's were surprised to see Miss Stewart's dog lying on the ground next to a big maple tree. They watched carefully from a distance and when after a long while they saw no movement, they crept carefully forward and discovered the dog to be dead. When this eventful news spread, there was a great deal of rejoicing among all the neighborhood children.

The move to the berry shed was much less exciting for Jean. In order to move their own house over the soft dirt, the movers had decided, the ground would have to be frozen. The berry shed was un- insulated. Jean gathered newspapers from all the neighbors for weeks and thumb tacked them up all over the walls, windows, and doors in an effort to keep more heat in the shed. A tin stove was the heat source, and the boys hauled wood on a sleigh from their property in an attempt to heat the little shack. Despite their best efforts, the shack was always freezing.

One day John Bruce found $10 in the pocket of an old coat hanging in the lean-to out back of the shed where the berry flats were stored. He showed it to his Mom and asked if they could go into town to go shopping. He had great plans for that money.

"No," Jean said, "we will mail it to the Bodners for letting us stay in the shed."

John Bruce was heartbroken.

The older boys had a lot further to go to do the farm chores. There would be no baking in the little tin stove while they lived in the shack, so Jean had left all her baking supplies in the house. When the boys went up to do chores, they would sneak in the house and grab handfuls of raisins, nuts, or chocolate chips. When they finally got back into the house after months in the berry shed, Jean was dismayed to find her baking supplies decimated.

The ground finally froze, and the moving company came with a jeep truck to pull the house the 600-700 yards to its new resting place. This took a few days to accomplish. When they finally reached the top of the hill, the house had to be jacked up again and placed on the cement foundation. With the house in place, Allan was able to start building. The addition of a living room and two bedrooms would more than double the size of their home.

Jean convinced Allan to let them go back to their own home before construction was anywhere near completed. She had enough of living in the berry shed in the dead of winter. It would be at least another year until Allan and the boys would have a trench dug from the well to the new home site. Until then they would still be carrying water, but at least the wood furnace kept the house toasty warm.

Allan would work an eight-hour day at the highway department and then work another four to five hours on the house. Jean was convinced he was going to work himself right into the grave. One thing she was able to help with was the dry wall mudding; she said it was just like icing a cake. She had a real knack for it and did almost all the mudding in the addition.

Jeannie with the house moved to the hill top.

Men from the neighborhood and Jean's brothers all came to help whenever they could. Of Jean's three brothers, Uncle Morrie was the toughest.

Born Francis Morrison, he had only weighed 6 pounds (their oldest brother Jack had weighed 12) but he was tough as old cracked shoe leather. The boys looked forward to his visits with caution. He brought no presents, except pipe tobacco for the ponies, but to win his approval for anything was a prize indeed.

On one of his visits, John Bruce had captured a small green tree frog not more than half an inch in size. Thinking this might impress Uncle Morrie, John Bruce took it in the house to show him and the other boys followed. Uncle Morrie, Jean, and Allan were taking a break at the table for a cup of coffee.

"See, Uncle Morrie?"

Morrie put an arm around John Bruce's shoulder and drew him close. "What you got there, son?"

John Bruce slowly opened his fingers to reveal the tiny frog. Uncle Morrie jumped to his feet, knocking over the chair. He swore and yelled, "Get that thing out of here!"

John Bruce's eyes were wide with surprise. "It's just a little tree frog."

Jean jumped up to intervene before her kids heard a few more choice words. She shooed all of them out the back door.

John Bruce asked the question on everyone's minds, "What's the matter with Uncle Morrie?"

"Uncle Morrie doesn't like frogs."

Lanny and John Bruce stared open mouthed at their Mum. Robin and Ross began to snicker.

"That's enough!" Jean reprimanded the two older boys. "Now, no—more—frogs in the house. Is that clear?"

Jean turned and went inside where Allan and Morrie were having a nervous chuckle at the table. The boys stared at each other in wonder. Their littlest brother had just taken down Uncle Morrie with a tree frog.

By early summer, the main addition was finished and the doorway was cut from the kitchen into the new living room. Allan was still working on the attic bedroom for the younger two boys, so their brown wooden bunk bed was set up temporarily in the new living room. John Bruce, after using the bathroom each night, would come running full out down the hall, across the kitchen and living room, and make a flying leap into the bottom bunk. This, of course, was because of the monster that inhabited the dark space under his bed. One night while he was in the bathroom, Lanny placed a folded wooden chair under John Bruce's covers. He climbed into the top bunk, giggling, and waited in joyful expectation. He was not disappointed in the ensuing pandemonium. Lanny would grow up to love a trick as much as his Daddy did.

The Irwin kids with the Peebles cousins Shirley, Stan and Johnny.

John and Lanny somehow got the sadistic idea that summer that Jeannie had too many dolls, so to cut down on the population, they took a few outside and first drowned them in the rain barrel and then hung them, by their necks, on the barbed wire fence. Jean was quick to rescue the dolls before Jeannie saw this horrific act, and the boys received a stern enough punishment never to attempt infanticide again.

The Bruckal's were the only other family on Nelson Road with a daughter anywhere near Jeannie's age. Though she was two years older, she and Jeannie became inseparable. Terry loved horses, and so coming to play always meant a visit to the pasture. The stallion, Chester, that Allan had brought home from Whidbey Island was a beautiful pony but as mean as Miss Stewart's dog. They always kept a respectable distance from him unless Allan was around to control him.

The two little girls let themselves in the pasture gate and headed towards Chester's corral. He was so vicious he had to be separated from the other animals. Somehow, he had gotten out of the corral and into the pasture. Terry spied him first. She pointed and cried out, "Oh, oh!"

The girls both turned and fled back towards the gate, but they were no match for Chester. They could hear him gaining. His white main and tail flying, he was snorting with rage. The girls realized they would never outrun him, so they instinctively headed to a close by, four-foot high stump and clambered to the top. Chester circled the stump, furiously shaking his head and whinnying.

Jeannie began to call out in terror, "Mummy, Mummy!"

Jean eventually heard them and came to the rescue. Wielding a stout stick, she drove off the incensed pony and escorted two tearful girls back through the pasture gate.

The new addition to the house covered one of the old windows in the boy's room and Allan had taken out the glass but had not yet closed up the window with boards. The three younger kids, Lanny, John Bruce, and Jeannie, found one day they could climb on the top of Robin's bunk bed, squeeze between the bed and the wall, and, standing on the window ledge, jump down through the "window" onto their parent's bed in the next room. They had not even noticed all Jean's newly folded laundry piled on the bed. She had left it there to put away after she had dinner started.

A shriek from Jean stopped them on their third run through the kitchen. Retracing their steps, they peeked through her bedroom door and saw the no longer folded laundry strewn all over the floor. Jean sat down in her rocker and cried. Jeannie was unsure how to react to this unusual turn of events. She looked to her brothers. Lanny put his hands in his pockets and stared at the floor. John Bruce stared back at Jeannie then, following Lanny's lead, stuffed his hands in his pockets. Jeannie was bereft of pockets. She folded her arms behind her back and sadly watched her mother cry.

They heard the back door open and shut and their father whistling a merry tune. Jeannie ran to greet him and watched him remove his coat, hat and boots. "Mummy's crying," she blurted out.

"What happened?"

Jeannie put one finger in her mouth and shrugged.

It did not take Allan more than a moment to assess the situation. He loudly instructed the kids to refold the laundry and took Jean out for a walk down Nelson Road.

"Why is life always so hard, Allan?"

"Things will look better in the morning." Whistling, he took her hand and gently swung it as they walked.

Coming back up the road, at twilight, they rounded the bend in the road and looked up to see their house, every newly installed electric light shining, at the top of the hill. They could hear the kids shrieking and laughing. Sparky laid guard on the front porch, watching for them.

"What do you think, Jean?"

She leaned her head against his shoulder and they stood for a moment on the gravel road. "Its perfect, isn't it, Allan."

Epilogue

Jean and Allan sold their beloved farm in April of 1985 and moved to a lovely home on a paved street in nearby Abbotsford.

Allan and Jean both lived to be 84, but Jean outlived Allan by 18 years, passing in 2004.

While building a fence on their new property in 1986, Allan realized one of his fervent wishes; he died with his boots on.

Jean and Allan 1982 (Photo by Dennis Little)

Made in the USA
Charleston, SC
25 February 2014